THE LONG WALK HOME

LIANE FAULDER

THE LONG WALK HOME

PAUL FRANKLIN'S JOURNEY
FROM AFGHANISTAN

>>> A SOLDIER'S STORY

BRINDLE
& GLASS

LIBRARY AND ARCHIVES CANADA CATALOGUING IN PUBLICATION
Faulder, Liane, 1959–
The long walk home: Paul Franklin's journey home from Afghanistan /
Liane Faulder.

ISBN 978-1-897142-25-7

1. Franklin, Paul Milsom, 1967–. 2. Afghan War, 2001– —Personal narratives, Canadian. 3. Amputees—Canada—Biography. I. Title.
DS371.413.F74F39 2007   958.104'7092   C2007-902552-8

Editor: Linda Goyette
Cover image: Bruce Edwards
Interior photo credits: as listed with each photo
Author photo: Ian Scott
Cover and interior design: Jacqui Thomas

Brindle & Glass is pleased to thank the Canada Council for the Arts and the Alberta Foundation for the Arts for their contributions to our publishing program.

Brindle & Glass is committed to protecting the environment and to the responsible use of natural resources. This book is printed on 100% post-consumer recycled and ancient-forest-friendly paper. For more information, please visit www.oldgrowthfree.com.

Brindle & Glass Publishing
www.brindleandglass.com

1   2   3   4   5   10   09   08   07

PRINTED AND BOUND IN CANADA

"Though the way is full of perils, and the goal far out of sight, there is no road to which there is no end: do not despair."

PERSIAN POET, HAFIZ

1324 TO 1391 A.D.

TABLE OF CONTENTS

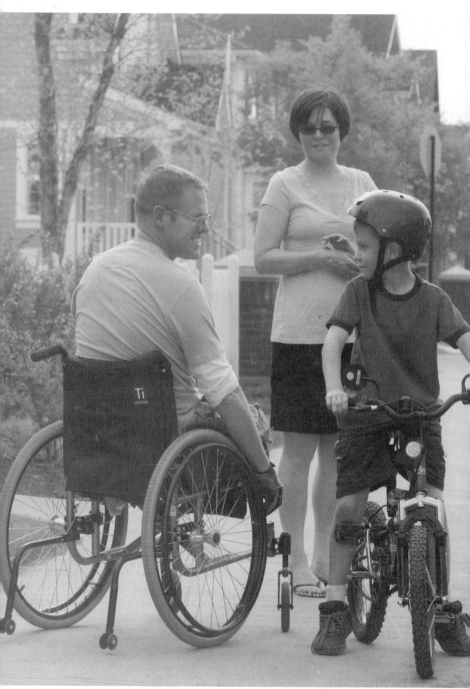

Photo credit: Bruce Edwards

INTRODUCTION

THE LONG WALK HOME: PAUL FRANKLIN'S JOURNEY FROM AFGHANISTAN is a personal story. It is neither an investigation of the Canadian military nor an exploration of the war in Afghanistan, although one soldier's experience can reveal elements of both. I set out to discover how Paul, Audra, and Simon Franklin rebuilt their lives after an explosion in a distant country tore their world to pieces. I wanted to learn what happens when a Canadian soldier goes away to war and comes back maimed. This book is about the courage of one Canadian family.

I am grateful to Paul and Audra Franklin, who reviewed my manuscript to make sure it was an authentic representation of their experience. The story takes place between January 15, 2006, and January 15, 2007. Consequently, some of the professionals mentioned in the book have since moved on to other responsibilities.

Readers also deserve an assurance of accuracy. I would like to explain my technique for writing quotes and dialogue in *The Long Walk Home*. I reconstructed some dialogue based on what interview subjects told me they remembered saying to one another during that period; these exchanges are not in quotation marks. Everything inside quotation marks comes directly from face-to-face interviews that I transcribed from my notebooks, or from video or audiotapes.

To put Paul Franklin's story in a wider context, readers can turn to Chapter 5 for more information about the war in Afghanistan. I gathered the research for this chapter from a number of news sources, including *The Edmonton Journal*, *The National Post*, *The Globe and Mail*, CBC.ca, BBC.com, and CTV.ca.

For the most part, I have referred to people by their first names rather than their surnames. This is a deliberate departure from the customary narrative style. The Franklins relied on a strong circle of committed Canadians—family, friends, and strangers—who worked together to help them. It felt right to reflect the closeness of these relationships through the use of first names.

I feel privileged to have had the opportunity to observe the Franklins as they walked down the road to recovery. I dedicate this book to them with the sincere hope that their journey brings them closer as a family, and leads them to a place of peace.

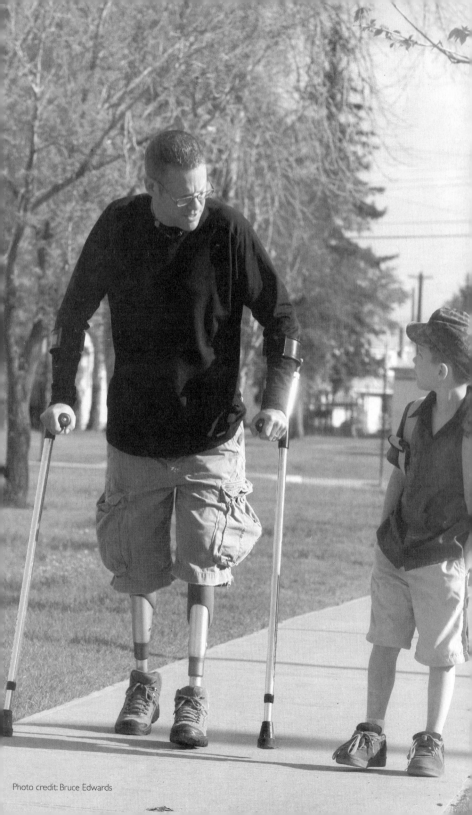

PROLOGUE

IT IS ONLY A COUPLE OF blocks from Master Corporal Paul Franklin's home to his son's school. This short walk through an Edmonton neighbourhood marks the end of a much longer journey that began in January 2006, when Paul lost both legs to a suicide bomber in Afghanistan. On that day, January 15, the soldier promised himself that he would do whatever it took to recover from his devastating injury and to reclaim his role as a husband and father. For Paul, that meant refusing to accept that he would live his life from a wheelchair. Doctors told him it was unlikely he would ever walk again, because few people who lose two legs above the knee ever do. On a softly green spring day, a mere four months after his injury, Paul is about to prove them wrong.

Wearing two artificial limbs attached with a harness to his pelvis, Paul steps from the garage of his home into the alley. His six-year-old son, Simon, is at his side. It is just after 8 AM and Simon has to be at school by 8:40 AM. Today they must be on time because Simon has show and tell first thing, and show and tell is Daddy and his new prostheses. Paul grips his arm crutches and takes a deep breath. This is his first day out of the rehabilitation hospital.

"Let's head for the front sidewalk," he says to Simon. "It's cleaner and there are less rocks."

Rocks and clumps of dirt, common in this new area teeming with construction, are hazardous to Paul, as are curbs, cracks, and children who fly by on their bicycles.

"You okay with these little dirt blobs?" Simon asks, pointing to some streaks of mud on the pavement.

"Yeah, but the step-ups are hard," Paul says. "I'm sorry I'm so slow, Simon."

"That's okay," the boy says.

They walk a few paces together and then Simon bends down. He has spotted a patch of clover in the grass. Digging around, he pulls up a tiny stalk with three leaves and presents it to his dad.

"It's really rare," Simon says of the clover. "It's close to the four-leaf clover."

Simon is chatty this morning, the way he used to be before the explosion that changed his family forever. He talks about wanting to go on a military mission, like his dad. Paul reminds him he has to be eighteen years old to do that. Simon thinks that maybe it might be a good idea to join cadets in the meantime. Since the explosion, Simon has suffered from headaches. He throws tantrums. He won't eat. Yet today, he is his old self. Simon is smiling, helpful, and willing to talk about his father's injury.

"I'm taller than you when I'm walking and you're in the wheelchair," Simon tells his dad.

"That's true," Paul says.

About halfway to school is an intersection, with traffic. They have to cross the street. Painstakingly, Paul moves from one street corner to the other while a car patiently waits. He waves thank you to the driver. He has made sure to wear a long-sleeved T-shirt meant for running, because it wicks the perspiration away from his skin. Paul doesn't want to wear a sweaty shirt in front of Simon's class.

His leg is hurting—a lot—but he persists. There is nothing else to do but keep going.

"It's funny in the real world, because you absolutely have to do things," Paul says.

"Now you're in the real world, Daddy," Simon replies.

When Paul reaches the wheelchair ramp at the school, he hands one of his crutches to Simon and uses the right handrail to pull himself along, hoping a different position will help him to deal with the incline, which seems extreme. Pain stabs through his right stump. At the top of the ramp, a teacher waits, holding open the door. It's 8:35 AM. They have made it to school on time.

At school, Simon is too shy to introduce his father to Mrs. O'Shea's Grade One class. Paul pulls the boy close and they sit together on a shelf at the front of the room. Paul tells his story, using pictures drawn with a felt pen on the whiteboard. Here is a suicide bomber who has a mad face and seven rockets strapped to his car. Here is a stick man with no legs who is saying, Ow, Ow, Ow.

One child asks a question: What happened to the suicide bomber?

Paul replies that the suicide bomber is way high, up in space.

Then show and tell ends, and Paul must begin to walk six hundred metres back home, alone. Simon worries about how his dad will manage. Paul just smiles and shakes his head. Don't worry.

Thirty minutes later, just a few doors from Paul's house, a construction worker named Rudi Winkelmann stops Paul.

"Are you one of the wounded soldiers in the news?" Rudi asks.

"Yes," Paul says. Sweat drips down his back. The morning's task is exhausting him. Although Paul wants desperately to get home and take off his legs, he stands and talks to the stranger. Rudi was a small child in Germany during the Second World War, and he remembers the fear of that terrible time. He wants to thank Paul for his sacrifice, a sacrifice he makes for "all of us."

Construction worker Rudi Winkelmann greets Paul on the sidewalk near his home. Paul says Edmontonians stop him often to express their appreciation for the sacrifices made by Canadian soldiers in Afghanistan.

Photo credit: Bruce Edwards

"You're welcome," Paul replies. "Thanks for stopping to talk."

People like Rudi stop the soldier nearly every day because they want to share his experience. Paul accepts this attention; indeed, he is grateful for it. He wants Canadians to know what it's like to be a soldier in Afghanistan, because he knows he is not the first one to be hurt, nor will he be the last to sacrifice a limb or a life in a distant and fierce war.

"It's not just my story."

1

THE ATTACK

>>> JANUARY 15, 2006
Around 1:00 PM, Kandahar time

PAUL FRANKLIN LOVED BEING A DRIVER. He loved being a medic, too, but he really loved being a driver.

For one thing, his vehicle was a freaking great ride. Swathed in olive-green armour and manufactured by Mercedes, the Gelaendewagen—known as a G-Wagon—was a five-cylinder, turbo-charged, four-wheel drive that went like stink.

Paul appreciated the vehicle's smooth ride when he was driving on Afghanistan's few decent roads, but the G-Wagon was most fun to drive when he was off-road, bumping along riverbeds that could go from a trickle to a torrent within minutes of a big rainstorm, or churning through sandy ditches that left less experienced drivers spinning their wheels in frustration.

Where else can you drive a two hundred thousand dollar vehicle like you stole it? This was one of Paul's favourite quips about working in the Canadian military. He could have wrapped that thing around a pole without consequences. Here you go, Paul. Here's a new one.

While it was a thrill to sit behind the wheel of the G-Wagon, it was also stressful. A driver had to be constantly alert, monitoring the road and weather conditions, and watching for signs of a possible attack by the members of two groups: al Qaeda, the terrorist organization responsible for flying two planes into the World Trade Center on September 11, 2001, and the Taliban, former rulers of Afghanistan who had harboured al Qaeda for years.

On January 15, 2006, Paul wheeled out of the Kandahar Airfield (KAF), headquarters of the multinational mission to rid Afghanistan of terrorists. His shoulders hunched with tension. It had been a busy day spent ferrying military VIPs around the Afghan countryside and Paul was tired and anxious to get back to his home away from home— the provincial reconstruction team (PRT) compound on the outskirts of Kandahar City, some twenty-five kilometres away. The PRT was part of Operation Archer, one in a series of missions launched by the Canadian military starting in late 2001 as part of its contribution to the international war on terror. The coalition's goal was to flush out the al Qaeda terrorist network headed by Osama bin Laden, as well as remnants of the Taliban regime that was officially ousted in the fall of 2001 but remainded fiercely determined to retain control where they could. Kandahar remained a stronghold for the insurgents—or the bad guys, as Paul called them—a collection of Taliban and al Qaeda fighters as well as militias run by local warlords, drug lords, and others who just didn't want international troops invading their country.

Travelling north toward the city, Paul accelerated. He noticed the sky had clouded over, which was unusual. Paul had come to appreciate winter in Afghanistan, when temperatures dropped from scorching summertime highs of fifty degrees Celsius to a pleasant thirteen or fourteen during the day. The winter skies were nearly always fresh and blue, with purple-grey mountains rimming the horizon. Today, rain had begun to spatter the windshield. Paul glanced at the others in the vehicle—fellow soldiers Pte. Will Salikin and Cpl. Jeff Bailey, and a Canadian diplomat by the name of Glyn Berry—and realized their moods matched the weather.

Part of the route between the airfield and Kandahar City ran northwest along Highway 1, a new stretch of road built by members of the international military force that had been stationed in Afghanistan since 9/11. Highway 1, a clean patch with no potholes, was the good news. The bad news was that the stretch had become known as IED Alley. IEDs are Improvised Explosive Devices, military jargon for the rag-tag collection of explosives, including rockets and artillery shells, used by insurgents to attack coalition forces. A bomb wired into a vehicle, often a taxicab, was increasingly popular as a means of attack. Inspired by the success of suicide bombs in Iraq, the Taliban and al Qaeda had added the technique to their arsenal, staging at least two dozen attacks in Afghanistan in the four months leading up to January 2006.

Remarkably, the suicide car bombs had not killed any Canadians yet. Paul wanted to keep it that way, and he was protective of the people he drove to and from military assignments.

Driving on the highway was somewhat less dangerous than driving in the city; there was less traffic and fewer places for insurgents to hide. That meant the atmosphere inside the vehicle was more relaxed, with more excuses for goofy banter. Paul had his standard lines for these rare moments. Look at that, boys. There's some T and A. He would point to burqua-clad women whose flowing robes revealed only their toes and ankles.

This day, however, there were no jokes. Glyn Berry, fifty-nine, the PRT's political director, was known as The Professor to his colleagues. He had rarely said a word on previous occasions when Paul had been his chauffeur. Today was no exception. The other soldiers were quiet, too. The only smile in the vehicle appeared on the face of Jenna, the small good-luck doll stuck to the dashboard. Paul had picked up the doll in California while on leave a month earlier. Jenna was a hula dancer, with a grass skirt and a cheerful, yellow lei. Personal accessories in the G-Wagon were, strictly speaking, forbidden, but Jenna gave Paul a lift and reminded him of his recent trip to Disneyland with his wife, Audra, and son, Simon.

ALTHOUGH CALIFORNIA HAD BEEN uncharacteristically cool and rainy that December, the trip was the best holiday the Franklin family had ever known. Simon and Audra flew from Edmonton, and Paul made his way from Afghanistan to meet them. Paul remembered getting off the plane and spying his wife and son in the waiting area of the Los Angeles airport. Simon was asleep in the carseat that Audra had brought from home. After a teary reunion, Paul loaded their gear into the rental car and the family drove ninety minutes to Laguna Beach to visit Audra's aunt, Joan Stratton, and uncle, Turk Timur. A few days later, Audra's mother, Faye Marshall, flew down to join the family and they all celebrated Christmas together.

Paul, Audra, and Simon stayed at a hotel near Joan's place. Paul and Simon, wearing jeans and sweatshirts, built castles at the beach, ignoring the grey sky and the cool and damp sand. Audra curled up with a book while the boys played, happy to abandon her role as a single parent for a day or two.

Turk, a Muslim, and Joan, an agnostic, generally didn't celebrate Christmas, but they made the effort for Simon. Joan bought Simon an avocado tree for their hotel room to substitute for an evergreen. On Christmas Eve, Audra "cooked" (ordered pizza) and the family decorated the tiny tree. The next morning, Paul gave Audra and Simon exotic gifts from the Middle East; Audra was thrilled with a string of creamy pearls from Dubai, one of the stops between Afghanistan and California. Simon clutched his new toy to his chest. The stuffed camel with soulful brown eyes quickly became one of the boy's favourites.

For Paul and Audra, the trip was a familiar mixture of joy and anxiety. The two had been apart for nearly five months; they felt like

Paul and Simon enjoy some time at the beach in December 2006 during a family trip to California.

Photo credit: Franklin family archive

strangers and had to make their way back to an intimate relationship. Paul was torn between listening attentively to every word Simon uttered and wanting to lavish his attention on Audra. Even as the family enjoyed each moment together, every sunset brought them closer to the end of their trip. Every special outing—to Disneyland, to SeaWorld—was bittersweet.

Paul thought of the goodbyes in California as Jenna bounced on the dashboard. Just one more month, he thought. He decided to try and reach Audra by telephone later. See you in a few weeks, he would say when the call ended. That would feel good.

Later, Paul would wonder about that day in the G-Wagon, the silence, the waiting. He wondered if the men in his vehicle had a hunch something bad was about to happen, an instinct about the danger that waited on the road ahead. A premonition would have meant there was a start to this crazy story, a way to make sense of the events that followed. In truth, Paul was not expecting to be blown up.

PAUL WAS THIRTY-EIGHT. HE HAD been in the Canadian Forces for only seven years, which set him apart from his fellow soldiers. Most of the men and women his age had either long ago become officers or left the military to start another career after putting in the ten years required to qualify for a modest pension.

Paul did not sign up as a soldier until he was thirty. He had spent his twenties trying to figure out what to do with his life. He worked in a shoe store. He went to college briefly, and decided it wasn't his thing. Eventually, he took a job in Vancouver, selling electrical equipment to building contractors. Not a naturally outgoing person, Paul hated the cold calls required in sales, and the constant pressure to be "on."

A tall, sandy-haired man with blue eyes and a wide, white, boyish grin, Paul loved a physical challenge. He longed for a more

Paul works with a young patient at a free clinic in Afghanistan in September 2005.

Photo credit: Reproduced courtesy of the Department of National Defence and with the permission of the Minister of Public Works and Government Services, 2007

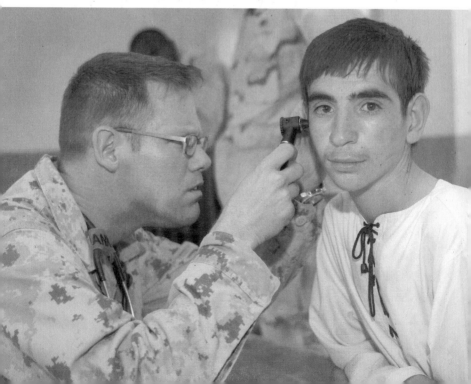

adventurous job, one that would push his mind and his body, and maybe offer the opportunity for travel. Paul's father had spent a couple of years in the military as a young man, so he was familiar with the tales of rubbing boots with blacking till they shone. After a trial period in the militia, Paul joined the regular forces in 1998. By the time he finished basic training and joined 1 Field Ambulance in Edmonton a year later, Paul was hooked on the idea of serving as a medic.

In Afghanistan, he particularly enjoyed working with locals during free clinics set up just outside the PRT compound. Paul liked meeting the women and children and was always amazed at how a small thing, such as cleaning a little boy's ears of wax so he could hear better, could make a big difference in a family's life.

The clinics gave Paul a high for days, but there had been fewer clinics of late. Attacks on coalition forces were increasing, and that meant the humanitarian elements of the mission—the clinics, the visits to local schools to deliver paper and pencils—were on the decline. Paul spent more time driving and providing security for a variety of military and diplomatic officials.

On the day of the explosion, Paul woke up after a tough night. He had slept badly and was cranky over his morning tea. He shared a room with eight other guys, all members of same section who were together pretty much 24/7. After more than five months in close quarters, Paul had had about all he could take of the snoring and farting that punctuated nights at the PRT. He had complained to Audra in phone calls. I'm a thirty-eight-year-old man and I'm sleeping in the top bunk, Paul said. It's ridiculous.

It was near the end of the tour and everybody was plain sick of everybody else. Paul found himself frequently on edge. He believed in his role as a Canadian soldier, helping to reconstruct Afghanistan after decades of war, but he was as much as twenty years older than most of the enlisted men and women around him. The age difference added to his sense of isolation and fueled his need to get home. Sure, they were only teasing most of the time, but Paul got sick of being referred to as an old man by younger soldiers who were testosterone-driven and anxious to prove themselves at every opportunity.

Paul carried 205 pounds on his 5 foot 11 inch frame and he knew he could probably afford to trim down a bit. He didn't feel the same need to spend hours daily in the gym, buffing his body to a fine sheen of muscle under skin, the way the young guys did. When he was at home in Edmonton, Paul—a gifted runner—pounded out between five and fifteen kilometres each day. Overseas, the days were long and hard. Paul preferred to spend his few free hours sending e-mails to Audra and Simon, or watching movies on his portable DVD player while in bed, waiting for sleep to erase the anxieties borne of the day.

>>>

THE DAY OF THE ATTACK STARTED with its usual load of worries. When Paul received his mission orders early that morning, they came with an extra warning: military intelligence had picked up the rumour of a planned suicide bomb attack on coalition forces that day. Word was the bomber would be driving a cab.

Paul did not know whether to panic or to yawn. Almost every day he heard another whispered tale of a dangerous threat to coalition forces, roughly thirty thousand soldiers from three dozen nations around the world. Rarely did such information stop any of them from accomplishing their assigned tasks.

Still, the Canadian military took all threats seriously. Southern Afghanistan, where roughly 650 Canadian troops were stationed, was particularly volatile. During the morning's meticulous briefing, soldiers reviewed the procedures to be followed in the event of an attack again and again. Officers decided to combine two missions on deck to shorten the amount of time soldiers and officials were out of the compound and decrease the number of people at risk as they all went about their duties. This meant that Glyn Berry, a diplomat for nearly thirty years, would go with Superintendent Wayne Martin, head of RCMP forces in Kandahar, to his meeting with Afghan police officials near Spin Boldak, on the Pakistan border some eighty kilometres northeast of Kandahar. Then the superintendent and the diplomat would proceed to the Kandahar Airfield for Glyn Berry's meeting before heading back to the PRT.

The extra VIP meant the convoy would increase to four vehicles from the usual three. Sgt. Joe Brink, the mission's leader, would sit in the first vehicle—the G-Wagon with a turret so a gunner could sit on top—and he would call orders over the radio to the other three vehicles. Paul, Will, and Jeff were next, escorting Glyn Berry. Cpl. Jake Petton drove the convoy's third vehicle. Cpl. Michael Kotuk manned the turret in the fourth vehicle, his eyes and weapon trained on the ground below.

By late morning, the convoy had already driven to Spin Boldak and made its way back to the Kandahar Airfield. The VIPs jumped out of the vehicles to attend to business, while soldiers in the convoy reviewed their orders once again. Paul grabbed himself a chai latte from the PX, the military store stocked with snacks and toiletries. Will, twenty-two, and Jeff, twenty-six, sipped coffees, and the three soldiers kicked the dirt while watching the US Blackhawk helicopters take off and land.

As Paul waited for officials to finish their meetings, he reached into the pocket of his khakis and pulled out a tiny Hot Wheels car. Whenever he went away from home on a mission, he would sit down with Simon so his son could pick a small toy to send with his dad as a reminder of home. Idly, Paul spun the wheels with his thumb and thought about playing in the sand at Laguna Beach with his son.

Around 1:00 PM, Glyn Berry strode toward the convoy, nodding as he swung into the back seat of Paul's vehicle. Paul crumpled his paper cup and tossed it in the garbage.

Break's over, boys, he said to Will and Jeff. They all piled into the G-Wagon.

>>>

ATTENTION BRAVO 4, CITY SPACING, IN TIGHT. Sgt. Brink's voice crackled over the radio of the G-Wagon as the convoy hit the city limits. This was his signal to all drivers to pull in tighter, leaving no more than ten metres between vehicles.

Up ahead, Paul could see the iconic arches, half-finished, which marked the entrance to Kandahar City. He felt his stomach tighten as he prepared for a change of pace. After two tours of Afghanistan, Paul had learned to negotiate with speed and savvy the hazardous city streets. These roads were hopping and noisy, with three-wheeled trikes, donkeys, and brightly coloured jingle trucks vying for the same narrow strip of dirt. Throughout the day, the bleating horns of taxis countered the wail of muezzins calling faithful Muslims to prayer. Paul had become expert at concentrating despite the numerous distractions—swerving the vehicle around pedestrians and motorbikes with four kids piled on. Anything that threatened to cut into the military convoy would be squeezed out of the way. If other vehicles moved too close, two warning shots would be fired into the hood. Paul drove about seventy kilometres an hour, knowing it was critical to speed through Kandahar, where coalition forces felt most vulnerable.

Even as he fixed his eyes on the back of the G-Wagon bouncing ahead of him, Paul scanned the street, first right, then left, for any signs of trouble. There can be clues to a suicide attack. A well-coiffed man, his face freshly pink from the razor, is one of them. Suicide bombers may perform hygiene rituals as a cleansing preparation for the upcoming trip to paradise. Somebody who is driving straight toward the convoy without paying attention to other traffic is another bad sign.

Brink's vehicle pounded past the arches into the ancient city of 329,000, with Paul's G-Wagon tight on its tail. It felt stuffy inside the G-Wagon, not hot enough for air conditioning, but enough to make Paul begin to sweat. Other drivers let soldiers in their vehicles throw open the door and hang out with their weapons pointed at the street. Paul was never comfortable with that. The G-Wagon was an armoured box. Opening the armour even a crack made it easier to toss a grenade inside. He preferred his vehicle sealed, thank you very much.

Paul checked his rear-view mirror as he leaned into a roundabout. All clear so far. He peered ahead at the upcoming taxi stand that he had passed dozens of times before. Yellow and white Toyota Corollas were parked in a line at the curb, waiting for passengers. Paul focused his attention on the right-hand turn just ahead of the cab stand, which marked the final eight hundred metres to the PRT. Almost home.

>>>

THE NOISE WAS THE MOST STARTLING THING.

The blast was so loud that it stopped becoming a sound, and became a feeling that everything was wrong. A rush of air seemed to pick Paul up and cradle him as he flew higher and higher. His first thought was that he had been in a car accident, but he had been in car accidents before, and they had never felt like this. He figured he must have hit something big, possibly a bus. He hoped it wasn't a school bus full of children.

For a moment Paul felt confused and worried that he was responsible for someone being hurt. Then all thoughts disappeared as the hard ground rose up to meet him. Paul tumbled into the dust and the dirt. Briefly, he was grateful because his helmet seemed to have stayed on. Before he could think of anything else, he slammed into a wall of mud and brick. He landed sitting down, with his back perfectly straight, as if he had chosen to stop for a rest. Paul sat still. Alone. Then, rage.

Fuck, shit, son of a bitch, he yelled as he ripped off his helmet. He tossed it, and the helmet bounced away. He was angry because he knew something bad had happened and he was going to have to fix it. He had no time to think about what to do next; he could smell burning hair. His hair. He reached up to rub his head, to rub his face, which was also burning. His hands burned, felt scorched, and yet, rubbing seemed to help. The flame went out. Paul felt somebody hit him on the shoulder, but when he looked up, he saw no one. Later he learned a fellow soldier had arrived on the scene and was shouting at Paul to get his attention. The wounded driver was silent.

Paul disappeared into his own pain. All around him, Canadian soldiers were acting quickly, as they had been trained to do in this emergency. Somebody alerted the nearby PRT and the Quick Reaction Force raced to the scene to provide security and medical care. Several soldiers formed a protective ring around the injured men and the smoldering G-Wagon, frantically working to rescue the wounded. Will Salikin was trapped in the vehicle, pinned under a load of medical supplies and equipment, including grenades and rockets. The explosion had knocked him out and left him with brain and spinal cord injuries and a shattered right arm.

Glyn Berry was dead. The diplomat had been blown to bits by the force of the bomb, made of seven 102-millimetre rockets tied together. His death would mark the beginning of a dramatic slowdown in Canadian aid and development in Afghanistan. Within three months, the Canadian International Development Agency would suspend its projects in southern Afghanistan because of the growing danger.

Thrown from the vehicle, Jeff Bailey lay face down in one

of the sewer ditches that lined the streets of Kandahar. He was unconscious and would not wake up for nearly three months. The bodies of two Afghan children lay on top of Jeff, two innocents killed by the explosion that also injured roughly a dozen Afghan citizens. Later, the Taliban took credit for the suicide car bomb—the first to hit Canadian troops—and warned that it was a sign of more violence to come.

Meanwhile, Paul—the only injured soldier who was conscious—began to act on instinct. He reached for the tourniquet he kept in his left pocket. Then he noticed his left leg was gone. All he could see was his femur, glistening white and wet with blood, sticking straight out from his mid-thigh. About five metres away, Paul spotted the rest of his leg, its bloody end poking out of the top of the pant leg. And then he saw his foot. He knew it was his foot because it was wearing his boot. Suddenly, he remembered the pain of the leg as it was ripped from his body. It was not like a break; there was no grinding of bones, no crack. The leg had been sliced right off, like a piece of soft meat.

Shit, Paul thought. I've got to fix this.

His medic skills kicked in. Paul performed a quick self-assessment, wiggling his fingers and toes. His right leg was tucked under his body, so Paul assumed it was okay. He could sense the toes on his left foot wiggling. This was puzzling, because the toes were quite some distance away. Paul moved his head: good, there was nothing wrong with his spine. He told himself to take deep breaths. In and out. In and out.

Paul wanted to sleep, and he knew this was a bad sign. Fall asleep and you will die, he said to himself. I told Audra I would be back. He invented the mantra that would propel him through the coming hellish weeks and months. I'll get back. I've got to get back.

Photo credit: Ed Kaiser

2

AUDRA'S EXPLOSION

>>> A FEW HOURS LATER

THE PHONE'S RING WAS SHARP AND insistent. At first, Audra thought it was Paul. It would not be unusual for her husband to call at 6:30 on a Sunday morning. Sometimes he called home from Afghanistan at odd hours just because that was the only time he had access to the satellite phone.

Wearing her flannel nightgown, Audra struggled across the double bed in the darkened room. She fumbled for the phone.

Hello, she said, clearing her throat as she flicked on the bedside lamp.

Mrs. Franklin? It was a man's voice, brusque and formal.

It's Lt. Col. Lennox. Your husband Paul has been involved in a suicide bombing in Afghanistan. He's very badly hurt.

Silence.

Is he alive?

A wave of fear and nausea swept through Audra's body.

Yes.

Oh. Okay.

Lennox said nothing.

Thank you, Audra said, and hung up.

She rose from her bed and headed to the bathroom, down a

short hallway in the family's tiny bungalow. The Franklins lived in the city's centre, about fifteen minutes by car from Canadian Forces Base Edmonton. It was January, frigid and dark, and even though she was wearing socks, Audra was aware of the cold hardwood floor beneath her feet. Drafty old house, she thought.

Audra brushed her teeth and walked into the kitchen. She was numb. She phoned her mother, Faye, who still lived in Audra's childhood home in a nearby community.

Mom, she said. Paul's been hurt. Can you come over?

Faye was an early riser who had already showered and eaten breakfast.

I'll just pull my clothes on, she told Audra.

It was not quite 7:00 AM on the day that changed everything. In the other bedroom, Simon slept, curled up with his stuffed dragon, Scorch. Audra, a small woman with short, glossy brown hair and deep chocolate brown eyes, moved through the automatic motions of an ordinary morning. She got dressed. She scooped fresh grounds into the coffee maker, poured in a pot of cold water, and waited.

>>>

PAUL AND AUDRA FRANKLIN'S FIRST DATE was a movie. He wouldn't share his popcorn, nor would he offer to get Audra her own bag. Audra grins when she tells the tale.

"The last of the great romantics, eh?" She chuckles at the memory.

Somehow, Audra and Paul moved past the popcorn incident. Three months later, the two were living in a small apartment in Vancouver's west end. Audra worked as head cashier at a funky clothing store in the giant Pacific Centre mall; she had moved from Edmonton to Vancouver for an adventure a year earlier. Paul, who was born in Halifax but raised in Calgary, sold electrical supplies to building contractors. The couple had no car and lived paycheque to paycheque.

"We were so broke," Audra recalls, in a voice that makes poverty sound like the best possible start to a relationship. "We had lots of Chinese stir-fry cook-ins because that was all we could afford to make. We had no furniture."

They found a little Korean grocery store on Granville Street. Paul used to go there on Fridays because that's when the owner had fresh flowers, and he gave Paul the old ones for free. "So I got flowers every Friday," Audra said.

Audra was twenty-three when she met Paul. He was twenty-eight. Within six months, the two were engaged. Paul and Audra travelled to Edmonton from Vancouver because Audra's father, Bill Marshall, was dying. Paul had only met his future father-in-law a few times, and he wanted to make sure he had Bill's blessing to move the brief courtship toward marriage. Bill gave it happily. The couple became engaged on June 29, 1996, the day Bill died at fifty-three after a three-year battle with cancer.

Paul and Audra share a comical moment at their wedding in September 1997.

Photo credit: Franklin family archive

On September 27, 1997, Paul and Audra were married. On the mantle of their home is a wedding photo. In it, Audra is doubled over with laughter, her head surrounded by a froth of white tulle as she prepares to cut the wedding cake. Paul is grinning in the photograph. He is looking toward Audra as if to say I can't believe she's mine.

>>>

AUDRA'S MOTHER, FAYE, REMEMBERED how peaceful her daughter and son-in-law's home looked on the morning of January 15th, 2006. It had snowed the night before, and the front walk was undisturbed, a blanket of white. In a few hours, reporters and camera operators would crowd the yard as word spread about the suicide bombing. For now, the yard looked quiet and safe.

As Faye slammed the car door, her toy poodle Cinnie tucked under her arm, she noticed another car pull up. It was Elisha and Darren Astle, two of Audra and Paul's best friends. Audra had called them after she talked to Faye. In his early twenties, Darren had been a soldier with the Princess Patricia's Canadian Light Infantry at CFB Edmonton. He had participated in military exercises with Paul and had a great deal of respect for the medic. "If you're a medic and they call you Doc, it's a really good sign," Darren said. "Paul was a Doc."

Darren left the military after the friendly fire incident of 2002, in which American fighter pilots accidentally killed four Canadian soldiers and wounded eight more while the soldiers were on a training exercise in Afghanistan. Darren had come uncomfortably close to losing his own life on the same training exercise. Still suffering from post-traumatic stress disorder four years later, Darren knew what lay ahead for the Franklin family.

Darren and Elisha had stopped by the military base on the way to Audra's to pick up Nancy Arnold, one of a clutch of local military wives who helped one another cope while their spouses were away on this tour. The small group made its way up the front walk. Audra met them at the door. There were hugs, but no tears. Not yet. There was too much to do.

First, the phone calls. Audra had already called Paul's parents, Ron and Barb Franklin, who promised to leave Calgary for Edmonton right after church. Faye's sisters and her brother were next on the list. Audra had been scheduled to host a home jewellery party later that day. The party was cancelled.

Darren asked Audra if she wanted him to wake Simon and tell him what had happened to his dad. Darren and Simon were close. Paul had asked his friend to take care of his family while he was in Afghanistan. Darren took that role seriously, spending hours each week with Simon. The two would romp at the playground, play fight endlessly with military action figures, or watch dopey cartoons on television.

"We'd hang out, being dudes," Darren said about those times with Simon. "I'd get him away from the girls and their shopping. We'd be video game buddies."

Sometimes Darren arrived with Elisha and told the girls to go for coffee. Audra would throw on her coat, grateful not to have to be everything to one small boy, even for an hour.

This time Audra said no to Darren's offer. She took on that grim task herself. She walked into Simon's room and squeezed past the bookcase of action figures, the TV and video game console, the table with the train set. She sat down on the bed and put her hands on her son's back, pure comfort and warmth in the nest of sheets and blankets. Simon looked up at her.

Daddy has been really, really hurt, Audra told her son. A bomb hit him and he lost his left leg.

Is he going to be okay?

Audra told Simon she didn't know.

Simon pulled back the covers and got out of bed. The mother and son went into the kitchen to get some toast and juice. Later that day, Darren took one of Simon's GI Joe toys and sat down to explain what had happened by using the doll as a model. He told Simon that his dad's left leg was missing and his right leg had bad pain.

Does he still have his hands?

Darren nodded.

Then he can still play video games, Simon said.

At 8:00 AM that Sunday morning, the second phone call came. It was the military chaplain at the hospital at Kandahar Airfield. He had more information about Paul. The soldier was just out of surgery at KAF's emergency medical facility, where injured soldiers are stabilized before they are airlifted to the American military hospital in Germany. The chaplain offered bare details; Paul's hands and face were burned. Shrapnel had pierced his body in numerous spots.

Then the chaplain put Paul on the phone. Although he was still woozy from surgery, Paul made a joke about his situation.

Audra, he said. It's official. I'm now Stumpy McGillicutty.

Audra has a dark and quirky sense of humour. She responded to Paul's quip in kind.

So I guess I get my way after all, she said.

What do you mean? Paul asked.

Well, I wanted an automatic transmission and if you don't have a left leg, you can't drive a stick anymore.

Paul laughed.

I love you, he said.

I love you, too, Audra replied.

She hung up the phone and then slumped to the floor in the hallway. Darren managed to get a pillow under her head and her mother covered Audra with a blanket, but there was no comfort in that. Dizzy and shaking, Audra felt her teeth go numb. She felt scared, as if she couldn't get away from the danger.

The panic attack, frightening as it was, was not new to Audra. She had experienced panic attacks before, beginning just after Simon was born, when Paul had to leave for nine months of medical training in Ontario and her life as a single parent began. Audra became a new mother and a full-time military wife within the same month. She wondered sometimes whether the panic attacks might have been linked to postpartum depression.

"I became a very fearful person when I had a baby, because there was another person I had to worry about, this little life I had to take care of," Audra said. The world stopped feeling like a safe place. Now, six years later, Audra's safety had been shattered again.

Before long, the doorbell started to ring and members of the military began to arrive. Sgt. John Hobbs arrived first. He was a fellow medic who had been running on the track at the base only an hour before. Now he confronted his new assignment—to be the assisting officer to the Franklins. He would spend the next several weeks stuck like glue to Audra's side, anticipating every need. John bought milk for the refrigerator, drove Audra to the doctor to get medication for her panic attacks, helped to organize passports. John was followed by the soothing presence of Padre Bob Deobold, and after him, a steady parade of soldiers from the base.

The visitors sat stiffly on the couch of the tiny living room. Faye attempted to ease the tension with gentle jokes.

You guys have got to stop showing up in short haircuts with doughnuts, she said. It's a dead giveaway that something is wrong.

Faye is a former teacher, always outspoken, and humorous. A bargain shopper and sewing whiz, she dresses in a casual but coordinated fashion. Her light brown hair is cut in a neat, fashionable bob, much like her daughter's hairstyle. A widow for nearly ten years, Faye knows how to enjoy an independent life, and she offered daily support to Audra when Paul was away. Her diary is full of references to her daughter and grandson. "Brought home four pairs of Simon's pants to hem." "Picked up Simon at 4:30 PM as Audra had a doctor's appointment."

Beneath Faye's take-charge attitude and ready laugh—surfacing even on this terrible day—lay an undercurrent of fear. On her way to her daughter's home that morning, she could not keep one horrifying thought from her mind. If Paul were to die, three generations of women in her family would share a sad legacy. Faye was fifty-two when she became a widow, and her mother was only forty-two. Audra was thirty-two.

What is going on here? Faye asked herself.

She thought of the day her father had been electrocuted while working in a mine outside Medicine Hat, Alberta.

"The police picked up my mother as she walked back to work after lunch to say Daddy had been killed," Faye recalled.

Then she remembered what her mother had said when Faye's own husband died.

What can I do for you, honey? What can I do to help?

Nothing but love me, Faye told her mother.

She hoped to offer the same support to Audra that her mother had given her.

In some ways, however, Audra was more accustomed to making it on her own. Raised an only child by two teachers, Audra had learned to play alone, to be independent, and to act like an adult among adults early in life. Her father sat on the county council in Sherwood Park, a bedroom community east of Edmonton, and he was also on the local school board. Both of Audra's parents were active members of the provincial Progressive Conservative party. Audra grew up stuffing envelopes for politicians and knew how important it was to represent her parents properly in the public eye. Good manners, good marks and good behaviour—these were the hallmarks of a child well raised—and Audra was definitely that.

"Because I was always with grown-ups, I was taught at a very young age just to deal with it and be able to be on my own and to take care of business," she said. She had her first taste of the solo act known as military spouse in 1998, when Paul joined 12 Medical Company in Vancouver as a reservist and spent most of the summer away on basic training. Audra and Paul had been married the previous September. They were living in Vancouver, enjoying life as newlyweds. It was fun, it was romantic, and now, Audra had complained to her mother, it was over. In conversations that were typical of their relationship—close, but brutally honest—Faye listened carefully to her daughter before replying.

Well, you can sit at home and feel sorry for yourself and blubber and drive everybody away, Faye said. Or you can get on with life and have something to talk about when you get together again.

Her message clicked. From then on, Audra refused to stay in a state of suspended animation when Paul was away. This proved practical because in the eight years Paul was in the military before being injured, he was away from home—if you added up all the weeks and months—for four years. He never missed an opportunity to take a course or some extra training. Audra understood; Paul liked to learn.

After Paul's basic training, the couple decided to move to Edmonton to be closer to family. Faye lived in Sherwood Park, and Paul's parents and one of his sisters lived in Calgary. On Audra's birthday, August 29, 1998, the couple packed up their few belongings and drove through the Rockies. Paul joined 15 Medical Company at CFB Edmonton, still as a reservist, and then applied to become part of the regular force. Audra and Paul tackled a variety of jobs to make ends meet while they waited to become a military family. Audra worked as a nanny; Paul built trailers and pulled shifts in a convenience store. The couple lived with Faye for a few months when finances got really tight. Finally, Paul became a resident manager in an apartment building. That's where they were living when Simon was born on June 24, 1999. Just over a month later, Paul joined the regular forces and received orders to report to CFB Borden to train as a medic. Aside from a two-week break at Christmas, Paul was gone until April 2000.

After a few years of caring for Simon largely on her own, Audra found it less difficult to have Paul away than to have him at home. This is a common experience for the military spouse. Every time Paul came back, he had to find his place anew, reconnect with his son, his wife, and their friends, many of whom were not in the military. For a short period, just before Paul went away again, he and Audra had to loosen the strings that had so recently tied them together. They picked on each other, hoping the other would start a scrap. They squabbled after lovemaking, as if they were preparing to convince themselves they were better off apart. In time, they recognized the pattern and they were able to accept that it didn't mean they were about to get divorced. They were just doing what all military couples do: dealing with the separation the best way they could, juggling their intense need to be together with the reality that they would be continually apart.

When Paul first joined the army, Audra tried to avoid thinking of herself as a military wife. She didn't like the label, didn't like the idea that she was defined by a profession that wasn't her own. She rejected the stereotype associated with military wives—that they were somehow subservient, content to be shuffled from one end of the country to the other, living in identical married quarters, a pack of kids in tow. When Paul was first in the army, most of Audra's friends were outside the military. She spent her free time with girlfriends from high school, or new friends from various jobs.

Over time, she came to appreciate what a relationship with another military wife, or better yet, a group of them, could be like. The women talked about being "on tour" when their husbands were

Audra and her girlfriends make a point of being together for important occasions like New Year's Eve while their husbands are on tour. From left to right, Laura Gauley, Audra, Barbara LaPointe, and Marie Granados.

Photo credit: Franklin family archive

away, and in truth, it was like being on a mission themselves.

Shortly before Paul's group left for Afghanistan in July 2005, the military hosted a coffee get-together so spouses of those on tour could meet each other. That's where Audra met Barb Lapointe and Laura Gauley, two of a group of five or six women who spent a lot of time together in the following months.

Barb and Laura's husbands, Dominic and Mike, were both platoon warrants, a higher rank than Paul's, but Audra's new friends were down-to-earth women who did not wear their husbands' ranks. When Paul was hurt, Laura, twenty-eight, was in southern Alberta, visiting her mother-in-law. She made the four-hour trip home in three hours, driving straight to Audra's bungalow with tears in her eyes. Laura remembered the day she had met Audra at the coffee party. It was the third time Mike had been on tour, so Laura knew the drill. She stood up to talk to the others.

"I said, 'If we want to do something, we'll have to do it ourselves.' So I sent a pad of paper around the room and said, 'If anyone wants a support group, I'll make sure and keep in touch.' There was a bunch of us that said: 'Let's do it. Let's get through this together.'"

Laura was stepmother to Mike's children, but the kids were living back in Ontario with their mother, so Laura did not have the same child-care responsibilities as Audra. The two friends developed a comforting routine. On Friday nights, Laura came by Audra's after work and they spent the evening hanging out with Simon. Laura, who liked cooking just about as much as Audra, picked up ready-made burritos from the nearby convenience store. The women curled up on the couch with a coffee or a glass of wine, flipping through copies of *People* and talking until past midnight. Simon played at their feet, or watched a movie.

The women on tour always had a celebration when it was someone's birthday. From time to time on a Saturday night, one of them hosted a martini party, just because. Many of the women didn't have family in Edmonton, so they also celebrated important family occasions such as Thanksgiving together with their kids. New Year's Eve 2005 saw some of them at a new chain restaurant, Milestones, located in one of Edmonton's sprawling suburban "power centres"—shopping areas so large that most people drove from one outlet store to the next.

Nobody understands a tour like another military spouse. Barb jokingly explained it to her civilian friends. "It's like breaking up with your husband, but without the perks." By that she meant that saying goodbye for six or seven months felt as heart-wrenching as saying goodbye forever, in part because you worried about your husband's health and well-being on tour. If you had actually broken up with your husband, Barb chuckled, at least you'd be free to have sex with someone else. As it was, not making love for months at a time could lead to awkwardness at homecoming, which tended to go one of two ways for couples. "Either they don't make it out of the parking lot, or they're a little shy and self-conscious when they get home."

Many civilians offer a pat response when military spouses dare to complain about their partners' absence. You knew what you were getting into when you married him. This was a standard line Barb and the others heard over and over again.

"There is nothing more insensitive than that," she said. "Sure, you know to a point that there are commitments on your husband's time. We understand that. But at the time my husband, Dominic, joined, there was no physical war."

It took a long time for civilians in Canada to understand that life changed dramatically for members of the Canadian military and their families when the war in Afghanistan began. The last time Canadian soldiers had seen actual combat was during the Korean War. When Barb's husband signed up in the late 1980s, Canadians were proud of their role as peacekeepers—a model inspired by former Prime Minister Lester Pearson and developed in the 1960s. As tough as it was for Canadian soldiers to wear the United Nations' blue beret in the Balkans in the 1990s, it was nothing like Afghanistan. "Things were heated in Bosnia for many years," said Barb. "My husband was wounded in Bosnia. But Afghanistan is a God-awful place where horrible things happen even to the people who live there. That wasn't something I expected, ever."

Eventually, military spouses learned to avoid conversations with civilians about their fears. They shared those feelings only with one another. There were also many enjoyable times to balance the worries, days when the women giggled over little quirks about the tour that each had experienced. Laura remembered getting together one night after Audra had received a phone call from Paul from Afghanistan. He had forgotten his extra pair of glasses at home and wanted Audra to send them over as soon as possible.

"She was so funny," Laura recalled later. "She said, 'What is up with them forgetting things behind? How do you forget your glasses?' She'd make everybody laugh."

The longer Audra was a military spouse, the more she appreciated what it meant. It stopped being a diminishing phrase, or a label that meant she had no life of her own. It started to mean that her life was bigger than her relationship with one man. Audra began to realize that being a military wife meant being married to the military family. She was proud of that.

The Saturday before Audra heard about the bomb blast, she and Simon had run a few errands. They ordered pizza for supper. Audra enjoyed a giggling phone call with one of the other wives on tour as they shared some small incident involving the children. Simon was in bed around 9:00 PM after his nightly bath and bowl of Fruit Loops. Audra curled up with a murder mystery. Soon after, she fell asleep.

>>>

BY NOON ON SUNDAY, THE MEDIA had descended. Something about their arrival galvanized Audra. She decided to make herself available rather than to refuse to speak, or hole up in the house waiting for them to go away. Audra put on some lipstick and changed into a dark turtleneck sweater. Darren gathered more than a dozen reporters into the small front porch of the Franklin home so they could be out of the wind. Then he set up interviews, one at a time, escorting the chosen crew into the house, where Audra sat on the couch, waiting.

Faye ran around trying to find a good picture of Paul, because the media wanted photos. She settled on one from a scrapbook that Paul had put together from his brief tour in Kabul less than a year earlier. Later, Audra went outside and posed for the cameras, holding her husband's picture. She stood beside an Afghan flag that had been flying outside, along with a Canadian flag, since her husband left the previous summer.

Audra was eerily composed. She answered questions in a firm tone. If Canadian soldiers were taking it in the chin in Afghanistan, Audra wanted people to know the folks back home were just as stalwart.

"We decided to be the face of the military because we are strong enough for that," she said.

Coincidentally, Prime Minister Paul Martin was in Edmonton that day campaigning for an upcoming election. Darren issued a challenge to the media. The first reporter to get the Prime Minister over to the house gets the exclusive. This thought appealed to Audra. She wanted the Prime Minister to come to her house, to have a cup of tea with the wife of a badly wounded soldier. She didn't want to lecture the Prime Minister about Canada's role in Afghanistan, or cry on his shoulder. She just wanted him to see what it was like. He did not come, but rather phoned to express his support.

Looking back on January 15, 2006, Audra remembered the day as a blur, punctuated by clear, startling images. All day the telephone rang. The television announcers droned the same story with the same pictures played in a continuous loop. The names of the dead and wounded Canadians. The image of the G-Wagon blown to bits. Against that backdrop, key figures made their appearance and began to find their place in the tableau that continued in the hard weeks and months that followed. Audra remembered that her friend Barb, who was desperately allergic to cats—the Franklins had three—came over to help. As her eyes streamed and her nose ran, Barb put together a big pan of lasagna and kept everybody fed. When other friends arrived and asked what they could do to help, Audra told them. The bathroom was dirty; someone cleaned it. The car was out of gas. The coffee pot was empty. Audra needed a newspaper. One friend or another answered each request.

Around 10:30 PM Audra retreated to her room, although the last thing she could do was sleep. She had to lie down, to escape her feeling that she was on display. Somebody—Audra thinks it was Darren—bathed Simon and tucked him into bed. Somebody else washed the dishes, wiped down the countertop, and threw out the empty doughnut boxes. Finally Faye herded everyone out the front door and sent Paul's devastated parents, who had arrived from Calgary, to her home in Sherwood Park to sleep. Then she changed into her pajamas and went into Audra's room, where she lay down beside her daughter and tried to rest. CTV television was arriving at 4:30 AM with a camera crew to interview Audra for Canada AM. In just a few hours, each woman had to be up and ready to assemble a brave face.

Photo credit: Sgt. Dennis Power

3

THE OLD PAUL

>>> AUGUST 22, 2005

IN AFGHANISTAN IN AUGUST, THE HEAT is a separate being. When the early afternoon sun hits the black tarmac on the runway of the Kandahar airport, the suffocating waves ripple upward and become another physical force that soldiers have to contend with, like the fatigue, the smell—a sometimes choking mixture of diesel and human refuse—and today, the bone-weary sorrow.

Paul stood on the tarmac in the forty degree Celsius heat, one of hundreds of soldiers—Canadians, Dutch, British—lined up to say goodbye to four comrades in arms, four American boys who had died earlier that week at the hands of the Taliban. Nearby, an American transport plane waited, its giant rear clamshell door open, the ramp clear. Paul and the other soldiers stood at ease, waiting for the flag-draped coffins to arrive. Overhead, Chinook helicopters descended, their gigantic blades thwacking the hot air and sending great clouds of dust skittering across the tarmac. The choppers dropped off soldiers who had been patrolling in Afghanistan's mountainous Hindu Kush the night before. The men hopped out and scurried out of the way; nobody wanted to disturb the moment.

The wail of the bagpipes began and the line of soldiers straightened slightly, ready for orders. Two tan-coloured American

Hummers pulled up. Paul heard the clank of steel as soldiers heaved the coffins from the vehicles. An American sergeant urged the pallbearers forward, his voice muffled by the wind.

Battalion, atten-shun! The sergeant barked the order, and the soldiers carefully saluted. The coffins, draped with flags, moved past. Paul heard sniffles; the sergeant was crying.

It was Paul's thirty-eighth birthday. If he were in Edmonton, Paul and Audra would have invited some friends for a barbecue in the backyard of their little home, beer and burgers under a big, blue Alberta sky. Paul would have made a gigantic green salad; Audra would have ordered a cake from the grocery store. As it was, Paul had been at the coalition base at KAF for about a month. A birthday celebration would probably mean toasting his own health with a Diet Coke later in the mess tent.

Coffins loaded, the transport plane's ramp lifted upwards, closing snugly into the belly of the aircraft. The soldiers turned and marched away, passing the low yellow concrete building that had once served as the main terminal of the Kandahar International Airport. The ramp ceremony was over.

Dismissed! shouted the sergeant.

The soldiers scattered, their boots crunching along the gravel-strewn ground. Some headed toward their assigned duties; others took advantage of some downtime to hit the gym or rack out, military parlance for taking a nap. Deep down, Paul suspected the soldiers were sharing his thoughts as they hurried back to the land of the living: Thank God it wasn't me.

Paul walked toward his tent, a good twenty-minute hike from the cacophony of the busy runway. Officially, he had a day off, and before anything got in the way of that, Paul wanted to write down the day's events. Before he left Edmonton, his mother-in-law had given him a fat diary with the word 'Homespun' written across the front. Paul was determined to record his time in Afghanistan for Simon, so that someday when the boy was older, he would understand why his dad had been away so much. By the time Simon was six, his father had been working away from home for half of the boy's life.

The coalition base at the Kandahar airfield was located about twenty-five kilometres from Kandahar City. Rimmed in barbed wire and surrounded by desert, the base spread over a dusty landscape about 1.2 kilometres by four kilometres in size. By 2006 the airfield was home to roughly sixteen thousand soldiers from a number of the countries involved in the international mission in Afghanistan.

The base had a gym, laundry trailers, and a resource centre with video games, movies, books, and a coffee shop. A busy PX, or post exchange, sold American magazines and chocolate bars. A key component of the base was the multinational medical unit, which had several surgical suites and more than a dozen beds. A complement of health care workers, including surgeons, mental health nurses, and physician's assistants, rotated through the unit, where they tried to stabilize badly injured soldiers before they shipped them to the American military hospital in Germany.

Reaching his tent, Paul heaved open the wooden door of a white canvas structure the size of a soccer field. He shared sleeping space with about one hundred other soldiers. Inside, the air smelled of too many bodies. There was no privacy; some soldiers rigged up screens around their beds by standing extra cots on their ends. At least once a night, one of the beds, nothing more than burlap stretched across a metal frame, fell apart with a great racket, dumping some poor sleeping soldier onto his butt on the cement floor and waking everyone around him. Soldiers quickly learned to get by on little sleep. The bang of rockets landing just outside the base, or the shriek of turbine engines from Hercules transport planes, often disturbed their attempts to rest.

Paul walked to his cot, distinguished from the others by a barrack box at one end stacked with books. He ran his finger through the thin film of dust covering the paperbacks, dust as soft as talcum powder that got into everything, no matter how often soldiers wiped down their kit. Paul reached under the bed and hauled out his trunk. He rummaged for his MP3 player and his diary and headed back outside. He walked toward the nearby mess for a cup of tea. Paul set himself up at a quiet table, down at the end where nobody would bother him, and opened the book. "To Simon," he wrote on the first page of the diary. "Through this book may you see some of the things I have seen. Along the way you may discover some faults, but I will always be your dad."

Paul tucked the ear buds of his MP3 player into his ears and scrolled past recordings by The Clash, Tool, and Offspring. Today, he felt like a little bit of REM, in particular, a song that seemed as if it was written just for soldiers on tour—"It's the End of the World." Like many other soldiers, Paul had specific songs he downloaded to form the soundtrack of his life on tour. Up next was REM's "Don't Go Back to Rockville," sung from the perspective of the person left behind. Paul's all-time favourite, though, was the Bruce Cockburn classic, covered by the Barenaked Ladies, "Lovers in a Dangerous Time." As soldiers around him played Uno or crib, Paul listened to music and tried to explain Afghanistan to Simon.

"We have been doing convoy escort for most of the last month," said Paul in his first diary entry. "Moments of terror, moments of laughter, and times when complacency has to be forcibly shrugged off. Those are the times that are the most dangerous."

Paul's diary became more than a record of his daily experiences in Afghanistan. His notes offer a glimpse of all aspects of military life, revealing some of the core beliefs, relationships, and experiences of Canadian soldiers, and hinting at what keeps them committed to a career that demands great personal sacrifices.

At least two kinds of people enter the military: those escaping something else, and those who feel drawn toward the vocation, often through a family connection. Paul entered the military because nothing else he had tried had worked out. He also wanted a career that involved travel, physical challenges, and a pension. Once he became a medic, he found his passion. Although it sounded simplistic, Paul often explained his commitment to the job by saying he just liked to help people. That sentiment kept him going on hard days in Afghanistan. Paul truly believed in the Canadian mission. He thought his efforts would help lead the Afghan people toward a peaceful future.

"Someday I may look back on this, my thirty-eighth birthday, and think about its importance" wrote Paul as he finished that first entry for Simon.

>>>

BY THE LAST WEEK IN AUGUST, Paul had moved from the Kandahar Airfield to Camp Nathan Smith, where he and roughly two hundred other soldiers from Edmonton made up the military arm of the newly formed Canadian PRT. Another fifty soldiers stayed behind to support the PRT's work from the airfield. Located on the outskirts of Kandahar City, Camp Nathan Smith was set up in an abandoned fruit-canning factory previously used by the American military.

Life at the PRT was better than at Kandahar Airfield. For one thing, the food was tolerable. Soldiers ate food prepared fresh on site by camp cooks. At KAF, the food had been prepackaged and merely reheated in the mess; it was routinely described as inedible. Paul loved the fresh milk and yoghurt available at the PRT. Living close to the city also gave the soldiers easier access to local market stalls overflowing with melons and pomegranates as big as grapefruit. The fruit in Kandahar markets came from the nearby Arghandab valley. Twenty years earlier, the land around Kandahar had been irrigated and fertile with fruit and wheat fields. After years of drought and constant warfare, it was a dusty, dun-coloured wasteland.

The Arghandab valley, however, remained a small but leafy oasis, a precious source of beauty and bounty for southern Afghanistan. Although it was once green with orchards of all descriptions, war had made it difficult for farmers to maintain their crops. Many turned over their fields to the lush red poppies that yield opium, bringing untold millions of dollars to Afghan drug lords.

Local entrepreneurs also sold souvenir goods right outside the gates of Camp Nathan Smith. Paul purchased several small handmade Afghan rugs to send home as souvenirs. Bootleg DVDs of recently released movies could also be had for a couple of American dollars.

Paul's section had its own big room at the PRT, furnished with a fridge and five fans. The Americans had converted an old water storage tank into a swimming pool. By the end of November, when temperatures dropped to roughly ten degrees Celsius during the day, it was too cold to swim, but for a short time, the pool was a cool, refreshing way to relax after a hot day in the desert.

Living under one roof at the PRT were the soldiers and about one hundred civil servants from Foreign Affairs Canada, including Glyn Berry, the Canadian International Development Agency (CIDA), and the Royal Canadian Mounted Police (RCMP). The work at Camp Nathan Smith symbolized the Canadian military's strategy in Afghanistan, which focused on three principles: defense, diplomacy, and development. Soldiers at the PRT routed out the enemy. They also tried to help stabilize the region by providing security for diplomats and other officials who were working toward the creation of a stable civil administration in Afghanistan. At the same time, the RCMP worked with the Afghan National Army and Afghan police to establish a professional law enforcement organization and a national military force. CIDA staff members tried to begin development projects, including the rebuilding of a local school. Providing free medical clinics for the local population of Kandahar was also part of the job. Medics like Paul and his Edmonton buddies, Amy Pennington and Jason Pawsey, staffed the clinics.

The first assignment for soldiers at the PRT, however, was to provide security for the upcoming parliamentary elections, scheduled for September 18. Specifically, Paul's job in the late summer and early fall was to drive various VIPs around the Kandahar area as they worked with locals to help prepare for the elections.

Paul was on his second tour of Afghanistan. At the tail end of 2004, he had spent two months posted at the Canadian military's Camp Julien, located in Kabul, on what was known as a TAV, or technical assistance visit. As a medic, he had a specialty. That meant he could be called into Afghanistan to help out for a short period of time—a maximum of two months—and still be eligible for a full six-month tour later on. Paul's tour in Kabul gave him a new understanding of the people who lived there. For a month, he travelled with a team of Canadian soldiers embedded with the Afghan army. His job was to pass on first aid training to the Afghan soldiers, as well as be available to help Canadians who might be injured. Sometimes the soldiers and Afghan army members camped out in the mountains, and nightly, the Afghans would take the Canadians to drink tea in their commander's hut. The Canadians would trade potato chips for spicy chicken kebabs. Paul enjoyed the experience and was not unhappy to be posted to Afghanistan again, less than a year later.

Through his diary, Paul wanted to give Simon some idea of his day-to-day life, largely made up of patrols, patrols, and more patrols. Some days, Paul headed out by 7:00 AM for a twelve-hour round trip between the PRT and nearby villages or Afghan army outposts. These day-long trips would see Paul bouncing his G-Wagon along primitive roads between villages, occasionally having to cross the Arghandab, more a trickle than a river, but tricky driving nonetheless. Other days, he might be part of a short, routine ground patrol of Kandahar City, where the air was always acrid with the smell of smoldering plastic and other materials that locals burned to heat their homes and cook their food.

City driving was hazardous. In his diary, Paul told Simon: "Over the last few patrols, we have been hit by rock-throwing kids and teenagers. Two of the sections have had their rear un-armoured windows broken from large rocks. When the rocks hit, it sometimes sounds like bullets hitting the truck."

Another day, Paul wrote: "We drive, cut people off, give hard stares to the people that look down on us, we wave at the kids, imagine what's under a burqua, and try to avoid an overloaded, broken-down, reject Mercedes jingle truck as it comes straight at us. Really just another day."

When he wasn't driving endless street patrols, Paul was

The military is a constant presence on the tumultuous streets of Kandahar City.

Photo credit: Sgt. Dennis Power

manning the PRT's unit medical service during "sick parade." That's when soldiers with a variety of complaints, frequently gastro-intestinal, showed up for treatment by staff in the unit clinic, including a doctor, a physician's assistant, and a medic. Medics in the military are equipped with a wide range of skills, from tactical medicine—treating injured soldiers on the battlefield—to assisting the clinic doctor with surgery, running IVs, or performing small procedures solo, such as removing a mole. Days in the clinic had a rhythm, and it was staccato. In one six-week period, Paul recorded seeing 270 patients, at least a hundred of them suffering from a stomach flu. Occasionally, a local would show up at the unit clinic. Paul remembered a twelve-year-old Afghan girl with a bad cooking-oil burn on her thigh. She needed a skin graft, and her father didn't want her to have it. That bothered Paul. He and the other medics talked to the father and eventually convinced him that a skin graft would make the girl a better prospect when it came time for her to be married. It was the only way to appeal to the child's father; girls seemed to be little more than a commodities in Afghanistan. American surgeons at KAF performed the procedure.

Amy Pennington was one of fewer than a dozen women at Camp Nathan Smith. Sometimes Paul asked her to write to Simon in the diary. Amy was a tiny, soft-spoken woman of twenty-four, nicknamed "Mouse" when she entered basic training at eighteen. Through her years in the military, Amy had gained confidence—not just in her skills as a medic, but in her ability to think fast, always have a B plan, and know what to do when things went crazy— essential skills drummed into the brains of all soldiers. Amy also had a good sense of humour that she shared with Simon.

"There are wild cats in camp, but even though they are so friendly and nice, they are infested with fleas," she wrote to him in one entry. "One of the engineers named Fiesel petted a cat, got some fleas, and now they call him Fleasal."

Amy also told Simon about one of the soldiers in camp who had an unusual hobby.

"He skins mice, tans their hides, and uses them to make elegant sails for tiny ships he builds, or clothes for his Dungeons and Dragons figurines. He's right out of 'er. I have a good section, though. The other guys are great and we all mostly look out for each other."

>>>

THE DAY OF THE ELECTION, PAUL started work at 4:00 AM. He drove the streets of Kandahar in three separate patrols. The last one started at 2:00 PM. In between patrols, soldiers had an hour's rest and then were on call with the Quick Reaction Force (QRF), a stand-by crew that was always ready to leave the camp at a moment's notice to respond to an incident involving Canadian

Two Afghani children perch atop a bundle of wheat while riding a donkey through the dusty countryside near Kandahar.

Photo credit: Franklin family archive

troops, anything from a land-mine explosion to a car accident. After his assignments, Paul grabbed something to eat at the mess. By the time he chowed down on a meal of pasta, cereal, and fruit, he was exhausted, his shoulders aching from hunching over the wheel, his butt numb from hours in the G-Wagon. Still, after he shoved aside his plate, Paul opened his diary and started to write. The election had gone well, with no visible attempts in Kandahar to disrupt the voting. Paul wanted to tell Simon all about it.

"To our surprise, nothing happened," he reported to his son. "The Afghan National Army and the police closed the city to traffic. Only those cars with yellow cards were allowed to enter. By the sound of it, the Afghans have done a good job. This was their show, not ours."

After the elections, the pace of life at Camp Nathan Smith slowed down somewhat. Paul had more time for two of his favourite activities, reading and running. Often, he ran with Jason Pawsey, a medic ten years his junior. The two would circle 'round and 'round the inside perimeter of the PRT, roughly seven hundred metres. If Paul was the kind of soldier who joined the military to escape a career going nowhere, Jason was the kind who had it in his blood. His grandfather had been a prisoner of war in Hong Kong during the Second World War, and Jason grew up attending Remembrance Day ceremonies with his grandfather.

"He didn't talk much about his wartime experience, but the tears were in his eyes at every ceremony," Jason recalled. "You felt a sense of honour to be there, and I wanted to feel that as part of the military."

Paul and Jason met in 1999, when they were on course at Canadian Forces Base Borden. They were both posted back at 1 Field Ambulance when their medic training ended. The two hit it off, although in many ways, they were different. Jason hooted over football on television, while Paul liked a quiet game of chess.

Jason pored over magazines like Maxim or Men's Health, while Paul preferred books of military history and trivia.

"Paul was into books and useless information. If I went on Who Wants to be a Millionaire, he'd be my first lifeline," Jason joked.

Their rooms were beside each other at the PRT, and they spent a lot of time just hanging out. The two became master corporals together on the same day, January 5, 2006. A point system determined the promotions. Paul and Jason ranked in the top ten among medics across Canada who were up for the master corporal's rank. Jason thought of Paul as a mentor. He asked him for advice on everything from work to romance.

"You can tell Paul anything. If you have a bad day, you can talk to Paul and he'll make you feel better about your decision in a couple of minutes. And Paul will tell it how it is, too. A lot of his supervisors in the past didn't like that, but that's Paul. Paul did what Paul thought was right, and he lived by it. Paul doesn't ask permission; he's one to ask forgiveness later down the road."

Paul was confident to a fault. One night during their training at CFB Borden, a few of the medics-to-be got together at a party. During a night of hard drinking, one of the medics got mad at Paul and hit him over the head with a liquor bottle. The medic, a woman, cut her hand in the process, and it needed stitches. It was late, people were drunk, and driving wasn't an option. So Paul, who had learned suturing that day, offered to stitch up the woman's cut without the benefit of an anesthetic. She agreed. After sterilizing the wound with a slosh of rye whiskey, Paul tried out his new skills. Two days later, the woman was at the Borden medical clinic with an infection in the wound.

"That was Paul. I called him the mad doctor. He was ready, no matter what happened; if he didn't have the supplies, he would think of something."

Jason knew that sometimes Paul's ideas were "out there." Even if he didn't think Paul was right, Jason always admired his enthusiasm.

"He might have an idea of a better bandage for controlling bleeding, some quirky way that I wouldn't necessarily agree with. But he'd try it out and then wait to get shit on for using it that way. He didn't really care. It was his way, and in his mind, it was the best way, regardless of whether his chain of command went for it or not."

Paul's willpower surfaced early in his life. Born Paul Milsom Franklin on August 22, 1967, in Halifax, Nova Scotia, he was the only son of Ron, a salesman for a pipe coating company, and Barb, a homemaker. He was one of three children—an older sister named Janice, and a twin sister, Nancy. Paul's mother described the twins as "passive" and Janice as "bossy," but the three of them were never any trouble.

Barb recalled Paul's childhood as she poured coffee into china cups at the dining room table of the couple's southwest Calgary home. "Paul and Nancy always had each other and it was much easier than having a single child. Janice, being the oldest, played with two dolls while I looked after the twins when it was time for feeding. We'd go for a walk every day and Janice would take her two along. One was a monkey."

In 1971 the family moved to Calgary, where the children grew up in a familiar Alberta pattern. The Franklins put church at the centre of every week, but sports were also important. Ron described their family as "very competitive." Everybody skied and golfed, and Paul, a natural athlete, also played hockey. His parents said Paul often pushed his physical limits. He was a risk-taker who tackled ski runs that were too advanced for him. Sometimes he got hurt as a result.

Paul joined Scouts as a Cub early on and stayed with the group straight through his teen years. The Franklins enjoyed many outdoor activities together, but Barb attributes her son's love of the wilderness and adventure to those early years of hiking, camping, and canoeing with the Scout troop. During one Cub event, Paul's folks had a glimpse of their son's independence. Every year in Calgary, the Scouts hosted a chuckwagon race at a local arena. Paul, who was around eight years old at the time, was supposed to catch a ride home from the event with another family, but there was some confusion. Paul was left behind at the arena long after the races ended. His parents began to worry when he didn't show up at home. Barb phoned other Scout parents. Ron drove around in the car, looking for the boy. Eventually, an unfamiliar vehicle pulled up at the curb and Paul clambered out. When the boy realized his ride had left without him, he decided to walk home. It was fall, cold and dark by the time a kindly stranger spotted him trudging down a street some four kilometres from the arena. He was even walking in the right direction.

"He was going to get home on his own," remembered Barb of the incident. "Now that's determination."

>>>

AS THE TOUR IN AFGHANISTAN CONTINUED, Paul relied on his diary as a kind of counsellor, as much for himself as for his son, who wouldn't see the entries for months. Paul grew to like the feeling of the diary in his hands. It was thick, as big as a hardcover novel, and seemed like something weighty and valuable.

Paul congratulated Simon in his diary when Audra told him that their son had come home with a mark of 100 per cent on his spelling test. Sometimes, after he talked to Simon on the phone, Paul would head straight for his diary.

"I'm glad your first day of Grade One went well today. I know you had a bad haircut, but the kids won't make fun of you. If they do, then they aren't your friends. I have missed a lot of things and events in your life. But I hope when you look back on it, you realize why I did work so much. We will have a great time in Los Angeles on my leave. Also, after the tour, we will spend some time together. Maybe go to Banff and go bike riding."

In another entry, Paul tried to convince Simon, and perhaps himself, that being away so much was worthwhile. "Today was parent-teacher interviews. In many ways, I'm tired of missing firsts. But it's all for the greater good."

Sometimes the diary oozed guilt. When Audra complained she was having trouble with the stove, Paul tried to research solutions on the Internet from Afghanistan, but he turned up nothing useful. Audra bought a new stove. When his wife had trouble finding after-school care for Simon, Paul wasn't sure what to do. "Times like this I feel quite helpless. Audra is upset, and I can't be there to console her and that sucks. Days like today make me not want to be in the army anymore. It's the sense of helplessness."

Paul also let Simon know when he felt lonely. He wrote he felt badly that other guys received frequent care packages and letters from home, which Paul did not. "This trip in many ways has been hard. I had hoped people would write to me this time. I received one letter about a month ago and nothing since. It's tough—others get packages almost every week. I know none of my friends and family are letter writers, but it's still difficult to take." When Paul did receive something from home, such as a birthday card from his parents or a scribbling from Simon, he taped it into his diary. His favourite drawing from Simon was of two stick figures far apart from each other with a ball between them. The stick people were suspended against a big blue sky. Paul thought that Simon was trying to show him that even though father and son lived a continent apart, they were still connected, still playing ball together, across the world.

Paul was feeling wistful in one November entry. "I never thought I would find myself looking at the foothills of the Hindu Kush mountains. Yet here I am, away from home, away from family, my wife, my son. I own a sofa I have never seen. I have friends that have had babies they have never seen. Pride, honour, country—are all words. The more you are away from home, the more you see the good of home. Home sounds nice right now."

Yet at some level, Paul knew he would be bored if he were at home too much. He needed the excitement and sense of adventure of a soldier's life. He didn't get a chance to write about it in his diary, but just three days before the explosion on January 15, Paul had an experience that reminded him why he loved the military.

Raised in Calgary with easy access to the mountains, Paul was an avid skier and mountain "scrambler," a term that refers to climbing mountains using your hands and feet, but no ropes. It wasn't so much getting to the top that he loved, but working with the mountain to reach the summit. Figuring out the best route was a challenge for his mind and his body. When his section received an assignment for a mountain patrol of a small peak a few kilometres outside Kandahar, Paul was excited. He knew no map or helicopter tour could reveal

Paul proudly displays the Canadian flag after hiking in Canmore in 2005.

Photo credit: Franklin family archive

in detail how the enemy hid among rugged boulders. Soldiers had to walk in their footsteps to know what they were up against.

It was in many ways a perfect day for climbing, cool and fresh in the morning with temperatures just above freezing, and rising to about seventeen degrees by the time the troops finished the ascent. Though exhilarating, it was a tough climb; Paul carried roughly forty-five kilograms of kit, including his medical bag, flack jacket, helmet, and weapon, a C8 assault rifle.

"It was a big day," Paul said later. "I still remember climbing up that hill and how hard it was on my feet. I kept sliding and I'm old and I'm trying to keep up to these young kids. But I was enjoying it, too."

About fifteen soldiers climbed that day. Another section of soldiers stayed behind at the base of the mountain, securing the vehicles. While scaling upwards, Paul spied caves on this mountain and others nearby that Taliban and al Qaeda fighters had once lived in, and maybe still did. He hiked past the grey cinders of leftover fires. Some caves had been used as bathrooms, and still stunk. At the top, one of the guys took a picture of Paul. In it, he looks small, with a big helmet, and a vast world spread out behind him. A gauzy haze hangs in the valley, filtering the blue sky. There are no trees, no points of reference to stop the eye, just a sandy brown world that that goes on and on and on.

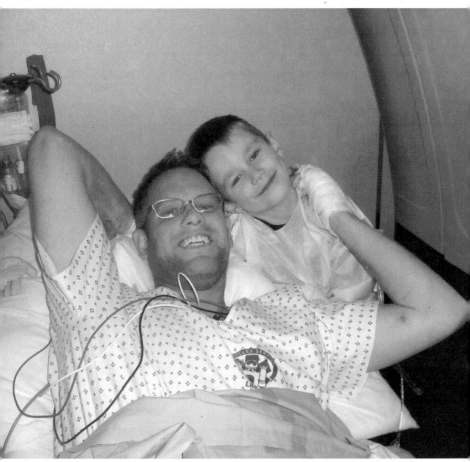

Photo credit: Franklin family archive

4

HURT HARD AND FAR FROM HOME

PAUL LOOKED AT HIS RIGHT LEG. Blackened, burnt, and broken, it offered a gruesome contrast to the white, crisp sea of sheets and hospital blankets that surrounded his wounded limb. Staring down, Paul felt distant from the limb, which didn't look anything like his leg. It seemed more like a prop for a Halloween party, or a fragment of a nightmare that had landed, bam, on his hospital bed. The leg even had its own eerie sound effects, like something out of a horror movie. The wound vacuum noisily sucked the body fluids that oozed from the injured limb so it would not be stewing in a viscous bath of blood and pus. The wound vac was connected by tubes to Paul's leg. Steel pins screwed into the bones kept everything stable.

Paul looked away from the right leg, swollen to elephantine proportions, and concentrated on the left side of his body. He found it almost comforting to look down at the flat, empty space beneath the blanket, the space that used to be his left leg. At least the left leg was finished, over and done, gone. The right leg, throbbing despite heavy doses of pain medication, was still frighteningly present.

It had been little more than two days since Paul arrived at the Landstuhl Regional Medical Centre, the American military hospital located five kilometres south of the Ramstein Airbase in

Germany, headquarters for the American air force in Europe. The largest American hospital outside the United States, Landstuhl served as a state-of-the-art medical bridge between the theatre of war and home for badly injured coalition soldiers airlifted from Iraq and Afghanistan.

By the time Paul arrived at Landstuhl, the hospital had treated some thirty thousand veterans from Iraq and Afghanistan, including more than five thousand with life-threatening injuries. Young men, some with facial hair still soft and straggly, hobbled and wheeled through the halls. Many had seen limbs blown off by explosions; blast wounds were the most common injuries at Landstuhl. High-tech body armour protected the core of soldiers' bodies, and the modern fighter survived warfare that would have killed soldiers in previous generations. However, in the process, they still lost limbs and sustained severe head injuries and horrific burns.

Landstuhl is located in a picturesque Rhineland village of the same name. A phalanx of surgeons and other specialists treat soldiers to the point where they can be returned to hospitals in countries like Canada, Britain, and France, where many endure months, even years, of repair work to their broken bodies.

Though Paul was still reeling from the physical trauma his body had borne in the last few days—he had already come through a series of surgeries—his stomach knotted with worry when he though about Jeff and Will. Both had been on the same transport plane as Paul for the trip from Kandahar Airfield to Ramstein, but neither had regained consciousness. Now, doctors were using medication to induce a coma in each man to give their brains time to heal. Both were breathing with the help of ventilators. Jeff was in the worst shape; doctors said he might die. Paul's friend, Amy, had stayed with Paul in the operating room during his initial clean-up surgery at KAF, and then had accompanied him to Landstuhl. She had been able to keep Paul posted on Jeff and Will's conditions. Now Amy was on her way to the airport in Frankfurt to pick up Audra, Simon, and Faye, who were flying at military expense to be with him. Paul pestered medical staff from time to time about his buddies, only to be told that nothing much had changed; both men were in critical condition with life-threatening injuries.

Paul, Jeff, and Will had been together for the bulk of their tour. They had eaten at the same table in the mess, slept in the same room, and had been laughing and cursing, bitching and bolstering, ever since they said goodbye to their families at Edmonton Garrison in July 2005. Now Jeff and Will clung to life, and Paul couldn't do a damn thing about it.

As a medic, he felt helpless. As a friend, he carried a sickening load of guilt. Paul blamed himself for putting Glyn Berry and his fellow soldiers in harm's way. If Paul had seen the suicide bomber, maybe he could have veered his vehicle in the opposite direction. Maybe if he'd driven a little slower, or a little faster, their G-Wagon would not have taken the explosive hit.

Still, Paul knew he was lucky to be alive, lucky to keep even one leg, lucky he was not breathing with a ventilator. Moment by moment, Paul calculated his losses, and then added up the things he had going for him. Okay, I am missing one leg and the other is nothing to look at. On the other hand, I have my arms, my hands, and my eyes. As he ran through the tally, again and again, another thought intruded. What would Audra think? When it came to balancing good and bad during the tough times ahead, what would her score sheet look like?

>>>

ON TELEVISION MELODRAMAS, THE WIVES OF husbands who have narrowly escaped death run down hospital hallways, their coats and purses flapping, their faces twisted in anguish. They try to burst through swinging doors, and are stopped by good-looking medical interns, who choke back tears themselves as they explain the dire nature of the situation.

Audra was not inclined to do anything like that. When she arrived at Landstuhl to see Paul, it was late in the evening on January 18, a bitter, drizzly night in the middle of one of the coldest Januarys on record in Germany. Amy had picked up Audra and Simon at the Frankfurt airport some hours earlier. Faye had taken a separate flight and had arrived first. The first thing Amy did was tuck Paul's dog tags and wedding ring into Audra's hand. Audra put them on right away, and kept them against her skin the whole time she was in Germany.

She was exhausted and overwhelmed. Even if she had had the energy to tear down the hospital hallway to Paul's bedside, there was extensive security. Audra stood quietly, her body quivering with fatigue, as guards checked her family's passports at the hospital's entrance.

As she approached intensive care on the third floor, a feeling of fear and dread welled up inside of Audra. She knew that once she crossed the threshold into the twelve-bed, highly specialized unit, a place buzzing with medical staff, she would enter another life. It wasn't the life she had expected, or wanted. Regardless, here it was. Audra realized she was not ready for any of this. In the three days since she heard the news, she had only been able to pack and get on the plane to Germany with her mother and son. She hadn't prepared herself emotionally or psychologically for her first encounter with Paul, because she considered the task impossible. It had taken all she had just to keep moving, to keep fear at a distance, to avoid all thoughts of an anxiety attack.

Audra?

A dark-haired man stood at the nursing station near the intensive care unit. He introduced himself as Nick Withers.

A member of the military for thirteen years, Major Nick

Withers, thirty-five, had received his medical training as a family doctor through the Canadian Forces. Last stationed in Comox, British Columbia, Nick had only been in Germany for two months. Strictly speaking, he was the general practitioner for two hundred Canadian families posted in Geilekirchen, some three hundred kilometres from the American military installation at Ramstein. Practically speaking, Nick became the Canadian military's point man as fighting in Afghanistan increased in the latter part of 2005 and Canadian injuries began to escalate. With a background in emergency medicine, Nick had visited Landstuhl several times as a liaison between military officials in Canada and the American doctors working on Canadian soldiers. He was also a kind of interpreter for the families of the injured men. His job was to soothe their fears and answer their questions, and to make sure soldiers received the emergency medical care they needed before flying home to Canada. He also dealt with the press. This would become one of his most challenging assignments, in the case of Paul Franklin.

Before the three Edmonton soldiers arrived, Nick's work with families had been relatively easy. But Glyn Berry's death, and the maiming of Paul and his buddies, marked an escalation in hostilities and an onslaught of fatalities and injuries that meant Nick's job became considerably tougher. In the four years since Canadians first arrived in Afghanistan in late 2001, eight soldiers had been killed. Within four months of Paul's injury, another eight would perished.

January 15, 2006, marked the first time a suicide car bomb had killed a Canadian citizen in Afghanistan. Though three other Canadians had died previously in explosions, the circumstances were different. Cpl. Robbie Beerenfenger and Sgt. Robert Alan Short died after hitting a land mine near Kabul in October 2003. In January 2004 Cpl. James Murphy was killed and three other solders seriously injured when an individual suicide bomber jumped on to their vehicle as they patrolled the streets of Kabul.

Nearly two years had passed without a Canadian battle fatality. In late 2005 the pace and ferocity of attacks against Canadian soldiers picked up. Nick was more than familiar with the big picture and the politics that inevitably surrounded a death or injury in the theatre of war. He knew that back home, calls for troops to withdraw would increase. These issues melted away in the face of each individual tragedy.

Nick remembered the first sight of Audra and Simon in the hallway when they arrived at Landstuhl. The young mother held Simon's hand. The boy had dressed himself head to toe in military-style camouflage clothing. He clutched a GI Joe in a clear plastic case. With two preschoolers himself, Nick wondered how Simon would cope.

Nick led the family toward a small waiting area outside intensive care.

No matter how much I tell you, you're never going to be prepared for this, he said.

He told them Paul was in serious but stable condition. While the immediate threat to his life, at its greatest on the street in Kandahar City, had passed, Paul still faced significant hurdles. Infection is a persistent problem in blast injuries and infection can kill. While Paul had received extra blood in Landstuhl to top up his body's supply, it was still not clear that the initial traumatic loss of blood had not badly hurt Paul's liver and kidneys. They can shut down after being deprived of blood. There was the amputation of the left leg, of course, but the right leg was also far from safe. The calf looked like shredded meat, and both the tibia, the bone which runs inside the shin and ankle bone, and the fibula, which extends down the outside of the leg and to the outside of the ankle bone, were fractured in numerous places. Then there were the burns. Paul's singed forehead was tight and red, and there was talk of skin grafts for his hands.

Audra and Faye listened, nodding, saying little. Simon waited.

Nick handed gowns and gloves to the family. It was time to go in.

Audra bent down on her knees before Simon, who was sitting in a chair, his legs dangling.

Simon, I'm scared to death to see Daddy. If you're scared, it's okay. You can be afraid, she said. Then she stood up.

Nick took her hand and together with Simon and Faye, they walked toward the intensive care unit. Simon entered the room first. From behind him, through the door, Audra saw Paul's hospital bed.

She walked into the room, covering her eyes with her hand.

Could you please cover up your legs because I'm not ready to look at that yet, Audra said.

She moved to the side of the bed with the least amount of medical equipment and hugged her husband, kissed him, feeling her throat tighten as the tears welled up again. It was his face. The angry red smears across his forehead made him look so much different than the man who had left home six months earlier. Paul grasped his wife's hand and then turned to Simon.

Hey dude, he said, desperate for a hug, but Simon shied away.

Faye intervened. Are you afraid of all these things around Daddy?

Simon nodded. Ever the teacher, Faye walked Simon around the bed while Paul began to explain how each piece of equipment worked. He held up his finger, capped with a thimble-like device called a pulse oximeter, and pointed to the nearby monitor, which kept track of blood pressure, heart rate, and the blood's oxygen saturation.

This measures how much oxygen is in dad's blood so the nurses can make sure my heart and lungs are working right, Paul said.

A nurse stopped to listen to the conversation. Taking the

oximeter off Paul, she placed it over Simon's finger. He looked up and smiled a small, thin smile. Paul reached over and hugged his son, who scrambled up on the bed and found a place to sit cross-legged near its foot. He hauled out his GI Joe, and Faye and Audra breathed a little easier.

"Paul smiled, he told a joke, and then we realized he's the same guy, just physically a little bit different," Audra said later of those first few moments together. "Then we moved on."

Faye decided it was safe to go in search of Diet Coke; Paul was addicted to the drink. Audra found a chair, dragged it a little closer to the bed, and began to practice a new lifeskill—simply going with the flow. Always a brisk planner, Audra soon realized that the organizational skills so valuable in her life back home were not going to be the skills that helped her through the next few days. With no plan, and no way to make a plan, she learned quickly to let things happen as they were destined to happen.

Amy spent many hours with the Franklins in Landstuhl, just sitting around, talking. Along with the other soldiers and assisting officers that accompanied Jeff and Will and their families, Amy played an important role during those hard early days. They were the storytellers, filling the families in on the lives of their loved ones overseas, and being there to listen when the families had their own tales to tell. There was a lot of back and forth as the military community drew a close circle around its own. Amy was impressed with how well Paul and Audra handled themselves.

"There was no use in looking at the past. Coulda, shoulda, woulda. Of course people suffer when something like this is happening, and we all cried separately. But there was no 'I hate God, I hate the world.' It was, 'We are going to keep on doing this. We're not going to give up. Of course you will get fake legs. Of course you will get a wheelchair ramp at the house.' The practicalities, that's what they were talking about."

Cpl. Amy Pennington meets Gen. Rick Hillier in Edmonton after flying from Landstuhl in January 2006.

Photo credit: Franklin family archive

BY FRIDAY, FAYE, SIMON, AND AUDRA were familiar with their tiny hospital world. Paul moved out of intensive care and on to a regular ward, and Simon quickly discovered the best vending machines in the area. Faye and Audra made a couple of trips to buy warmer clothes at the store on the American base. Audra found a German-style cuckoo clock to bring home as a souvenir. In the evenings, after a long day of talking with doctors, or alternately, sitting bored in a chair while Paul was in surgery, the family was grateful to return to Landstuhl Fisher House, one of more than three dozen hostels at military installations around the world. An American philanthropist built the chain of hostels to give families a place to stay when visiting wounded soldiers. At Fisher House, Audra, Faye, and Simon could enjoy a hot meal, such as a plate of lasagna, and a fresh salad, provided by a roster of volunteers. Games lined the shelves of a bright family room, and a computer allowed wives and children to write e-mail to their friends and families back home. A big-screen television was attached to video game controls by a nest of power cords.

John Hobbs, the assisting officer who had accompanied the Franklins to Germany from Edmonton, quickly learned that when all else failed, Simon could be soothed, entertained, and mesmerized with a video game. Audra had paid an enormous amount of money for the latest hand-held version during the airplane stopover in London, and John made it his mission to scrounge batteries. Once he tried to organize a play date for Simon with some other kids. Simon didn't seem that interested. Video games, on the other hand, were always available and gave Simon a way to enter his own world at will, a world in which there were no bandaged soldiers and no grandma insisting on homework even when dad was in the hospital and his Grade One teacher was all the way across the world and not even checking Simon's agenda book anyway. Simon complained when his grandma told him to do homework.

It's not fair, he said.

Life isn't fair, Simon, Faye replied crisply. Otherwise do you think your daddy would be here in hospital?

John figured video games were okay. Everybody needed an escape.

For Paul, an escape was more difficult to find. Each day brought a fresh round of surgery in the form of a procedure called an irrigation and debridement. Doctors put Paul under anesthetic and cleaned both wounded legs while investigating the surrounding bone and tissue to see if they had to remove dead material. Already, some bone and muscle remaining on the left leg needed to be cut out, making Paul's left stump shorter still.

From the beginning, Paul faced his difficulties straight on, with a determination to recover that bordered on flat-out denial. Even from his bed at Landstuhl, Paul confided to John that he planned to compete again someday in the Mountain Man, the military's version of a triathlon, with an extra event thrown in. In Mountain Man, competitors have to march thirty-two kilometres wearing a fifteen-kilogram rucksack. Then they must carry two seventeen-kilogram sandbags for three kilometres. A ten-kilometre canoe trip follows. The challenge ends with a six-kilometre foot race. Paul had completed the Mountain Man several times; his personal best was just over six hours. Once he did it without training, after getting out of bed on the morning of the event and deciding it would be fun to join in. Oh, he hurt, but Paul did it anyway.

John understood the nature of Paul's injury and the odds of Paul competing in another Mountain Man. He didn't dismiss Paul's goal. Nor did he humour him. John just listened.

"He said the leg wasn't going to prevent him from doing the things he wanted to do. Nothing was unrealistic to him," John said later. "When he told me his next goal was to do the Mountain Man, I thought, good for him. There is no doubt in my mind that he'll do it. It's just a matter of time. His body might give out before his mind does, though, because he's too stubborn to quit."

As Paul struggled to cope with each day's fresh medical challenge and his uncertain future, something else was brewing. Paul had been drawing strength from the way things had shaken down on the streets of Kandahar on January 15. In the moments after the explosion, when he saw the glistening white bone extending from his left thigh, Paul had pulled out his tourniquet from his pants pocket. Despite the chaos surrounding him, he had the presence of mind to use his medical training to save his own life, yanking the black band tight around his thigh, choking the artery and staunching the gush of blood. To Paul, this represented a triumph of sorts. Proud of his skills as a medic, he felt he had drawn on his training when it counted. As the black smoke billowed from the burning G-Wagon and soldiers scurried around securing the blast site, Paul did what he had to do. When he had first spoken to Audra from the hospital at Kandahar Airfield, he had told her the tourniquet story. He and others from Afghanistan told Nick Withers the same thing.

The problem was that the story wasn't true.

Audra had repeated it to the media in her home on that first day, and Nick had also told journalists about it. The tale quickly spread through newspaper stories and broadcast reports. It had taken on a life of its own, and began to include the rumour that Paul had dragged himself along the muddy street to try and help his wounded comrades. Soldiers who had witnessed the scene knew differently. Paul had not tied his own tourniquet; the person who came to his rescue was fellow soldier Jake Petton. Paul couldn't have crawled toward his fellow soldiers and Glyn Berry regardless of how badly he wanted to help. He was too injured to move.

As the conflicting stories found their way to Nick Withers, the doctor recognized the pattern. Paul had suffered a mild brain injury in the explosion. The brain had created the memory of the incident, and it felt as real to Paul as everything that had happened since. In medical terms, it is called a confabulation.

Nick knew confused memories caused by brain injuries were common after traumatic events, and that military doctors were seeing more of these situations among soldiers wounded in Iraq and Afghanistan. Doctors were beginning to discover that a diagnosis of post-traumatic-stress-disorder, with symptoms such as terrifying dreams and replaying the traumatic event, can be an error. In some cases, the symptoms may actually represent a brain injury. Modern imaging techniques such as MRIs and CAT scans are sometimes able to pick up internal problems even in soldiers who don't appear hurt on the outside, making it easier to properly diagnose brain trauma.

None of this would prove any comfort to Paul. Nick knew Paul was not trying to make himself out to be a hero. The wounded soldier believed with all his heart in what his brain told him was true. After making a number of calls back to Afghanistan to make sure he had his facts right, Nick told Audra about the situation. She asked him to relay the bad news to Paul; she knew she wasn't up to it.

On Sunday, January 22, one week to the day of the explosion, Nick told Paul the truth. Nick ranks the encounter as among the most difficult dialogues he has ever had with a patient, as tough as an emergency room conversation in which he told parents their child was brain-dead after hanging himself. He felt sick as he prepared to deliver the news to Paul.

"Here we had a guy who just lost his leg, being reported in the national news that he'd saved himself, that he was this big hero, and now we had to change that story. You've got a poor guy through no fault of his own, not a jerk trying to take credit, just a poor guy who has a belief in his head that occurred as a result of a brain injury. And then to have to go and change that. I knew it was an incredible blow at a time when he didn't need another kick."

It was a bright afternoon and the sun streamed through the window in the hospital room. Paul's face was healing, the burn on his forehead fading every day. He looked up when Nick walked in and smiled, as ever. His smile quickly turned to a frown when Nick began to speak. Paul's memories of tying his own tourniquet were so vivid, he simply did not believe it when Nick told him what had really happened.

At first, Paul was angry, yet he trusted the doctor, who had spoken to medical staff and military people in Kandahar about the story. Paul eventually accepted the facts. After the explosion, Jake, who was in the G-Wagon behind Paul's, ran to Paul's side within seconds. Pulling a tourniquet from his pants pocket, Jake wrapped it around Paul's left thigh and tugged it hard to stop the flow of blood. That quick action saved Paul's life.

After hearing the truth, Paul felt a rush of emotions. He was grateful to Jake, but humiliated to have claimed he had tied his own tourniquet. Paul worried what people might think of him. He was also disappointed that, in the end, he hadn't used his medical skills when it mattered to save his own life. Intellectually, he knew it wasn't his fault. Emotionally, he was crushed.

"I had trained people to put tourniquets on themselves and when the time came to prove myself, I didn't do it. I didn't do the job," Paul said.

Nick knew what that meant. Doing the job you're trained to do is one of the most important of military credos, a message drummed into all Canadian soldiers from the first days of basic training. Soldiers who do not do their jobs when it matters are not much good to anyone, and for a while, Paul wondered if he might be that kind of soldier. Later, he reminded himself that he had done his job as a medic in another way. Three days before the blast, Paul had snagged a handful of a new kind of tourniquet from the medical services clinic at the PRT. Called a Combat

Application Tourniquet, or CAT, it was made of a wide black band with straps and was superior to the standard-issue rubber surgical tubing Canadian soldiers normally kept in their pockets. Paul had given a new CAT and a lesson on how to use it to each of the other guys in his company, including Jake. Jake later used that information to save Paul's life. Thinking about that made Paul feel better, and reassured him that he hadn't failed as a soldier and a medic. He had done his job.

With that in mind, Paul promised himself that in the weeks and months to come, he would continue to do the job to the very best of his ability. The job would be different now. His new job was to learn to walk again. There would be no stopping him.

After Paul accepted the reality of what had happened in Kandahar, he and Nick talked about what had to be done about the

Audra travels to the airport on her way back to Canada from Germany in January 2006. Padre Bob Deobold accompanies her.

Photo credit: Franklin family archive

tourniquet story. Paul wrote a statement with the new information, which Nick released to the media. Audra talked to reporters about it and the whole family moved on. There was little time to dwell on such matters anyway; doctors at Landstuhl had decided the three Canadian soldiers could go home.

On Tuesday, January 24, about a dozen Canadian medical staff, who had flown from Canada for the medical evacuation, loaded the injured men on a military airbus for the long flight home. Jeff and Will were still breathing with respirators, so an intensive care specialist was part of the team. Paul no longer needed this kind of medical care; his issue was pain control. Doctors adjusted his morphine to cope with the ten-hour trip home. Nick came to the airport. He hugged Audra goodbye.

General Rick Hillier pins one of Paul's medals onto Simon's shirt while Audra looks on.

Photo credit: Franklin family archive

The patients were in the front of the plane, their beds bolted to the plane's interior walls. A curtain divided the patient area from the rest of the plane that held other passengers. Families and assisting officers could go back and forth, so long as they gloved and gowned before visiting the injured men. Audra, Faye, and Simon had plenty of room to spread out and be comfortable while watching movies in the spacious back of the plane. Simon sat in the cockpit with the pilots as the airbus approached Edmonton.

When the plane landed, the patients were loaded into ambulances and taken by police escort directly to the University of Alberta hospital, where a crowd of media awaited their arrival. General Rick Hillier, the chief of the defence staff for the Canadian government and the country's top soldier, was at the airport to greet the families even as the wounded men were whisked away. He pinned the honours earned by the soldiers—the Afghanistan Campaign Star and the South West Asia Service medals—on the families of Paul, Will, and Jeff.

Everyone was glad to be home. Faye recorded her feelings that day in her diary: "We came to Germany sad and afraid. It was wet, dark, and dreary. We were afraid for our soldiers and their future. Today, we left in sunshine with our hearts full of joy and promise for our soldiers' futures. God speed them to their full recoveries."

Photo credit: Sgt. Dennis Power

5

AFGHANISTAN IN RETROSPECT

>>> JANUARY 23, 2006

PAUL, AUDRA, AND SIMON WERE BARELY aware of events in Canada in the first weeks of their ordeal. They were immersed in their own drama. As they prepared to fly back to Edmonton from Landstuhl, Canadians were voting in a federal election that would lead to a new government.

Although Audra was a staunch supporter of Alberta's Progressive Conservative Party, she would have voted for the federal Liberals had she been in Edmonton for the big event instead of in Germany.

"I'm so political that it did occur to me it was election day," Audra remembered of January 23. "But I had other fish to fry."

Paul had voted in advance polls in Afghanistan, at a polling station set up in the mess tent at the PRT. He remembered that many of the soldiers grumbled that the Liberal government was not paying enough attention to reconstruction efforts. Paul voted for the Green Party. It wasn't a protest vote; he believed in the party's platform.

By the time the Franklin family arrived in Edmonton on January 24, the newspapers were full of the election results—an upset that led to a minority government under Conservative leader Stephen Harper. It had been a rancorous campaign. Paul Martin, the defeated Liberal prime minister, could not overcome the sponsorship scandal, or the public fury over the transfer of millions of dollars in public money to Liberal-friendly advertising agencies that did precious little to earn the funds. Martin resigned as party leader shortly after the defeat.

The Conservatives had promised more support for the military during the election campaign. Their platform included a commitment to increase the number of regular forces to about 75,000, as well as increasing the reserves by 10,000 members. (In 1990 there had been 87,600 soldiers in the Canadian military. By 2002 that number had dropped to 57,000.) Even before the Harper government assumed power, the Liberals had been steadily increasing military spending after years of cuts. It was the Liberal government under Prime Minister Jean Chretien that sent Canadian troops to Afghanistan in the first place.

As Paul confronted an ordeal of surgery and rehabilitation in Edmonton—and focused on his own recovery—Canadians were looking back at the escalation of a war they had never anticipated or clearly understood.

Two weeks after the World Trade Center attack in New York in September 2001, the Canadian government had pledged to support the United States and fight international terrorism with Canadian troops on the ground in Afghanistan. The US held Osama bin Laden and his al Qaeda terrorist group responsible for the World Trade Center attacks; the Taliban government in Afghanistan harboured bin Laden and his supporters. At first, Canadians accepted the clear imperatives of the mission.

When Afghanistan refused to hand over bin Laden, the Americans launched Operation Enduring Freedom, an assault that had the support of more than a dozen NATO nations including Canada, Germany, and Britain. The goal of the American mission was to hunt down and kill remnants of the al Qaeda terrorists.

By Christmas of 2001, Canada had already sent a small

contingent of elite soldiers—members of the Joint Task Force 2 commando unit—to Afghanistan in a mission dubbed Operation Apollo. In February 2002, the first major troop deployment began, and Canada sent roughly eight hundred soldiers to the south of Afghanistan. Most of the soldiers in that first round of troops were from Canadian Forces Base Edmonton, which had been next in the rotation for international deployment. The American government asked Canada to replace the battle group in Afghanistan at the end of that first six-month rotation, but Defence Minister Art Eggleton pulled the soldiers out. He said military resources were stretched too thin. Canada brought the ground troops back home in the summer of 2002. About thirteen hundred Canadians remained in the region, but few were in combat roles.

In the spring of 2003, the Americans invaded Iraq. The Liberal government decided not to join the controversial mission, but instead to send troops in full force back to Afghanistan as a signal that Canada would do its part in the international war on terror. Canada agreed to remain in the troubled country until 2007.

Stability in Afghanistan has never been easy to achieve. Located in the midst of a strategic trade route for centuries, Afghanistan has long been a prime target for aggressive outsiders anxious to secure the area. The Soviets were the most recent invaders, moving into Afghanistan in 1979 to prop up a communist regime. The move was bitterly opposed by groups of Afghan fighters, known as mujahedeen, who repelled the Soviets with the quiet support of the United States.

Ten years later, the Soviets finally withdrew, and in 1992 the mujahedeen captured the country's capital, Kabul, creating a new Islamic republic. By the end of 1994, the Taliban had emerged from an internal power struggle as the dominant force. The Taliban seized control of Kabul in 1996 and expanded throughout most of the country, spreading its version of Islam. Television was banned

Citizens in Kandahar City gather around a fabric market.

Photo credit: Franklin family archive

and women were forbidden to go to school, drive, or work outside the home.

American and British air strikes in the fall of 2001 made it possible for internal opponents of the Taliban, including the Northern Alliance, to oust the Taliban from Kabul in mid-November. By December the Taliban was also forced out of its longtime stronghold, Kandahar. At that time, the United Nations sponsored an international conference in Bonn, Germany. A group of anti-Taliban Afghan factions agreed on a deal for an interim government headed by Hamid Karzai, a Pashtun, the largest ethnic group in Afghanistan. Delegates at the Bonn conference also agreed that an international force should provide security in Afghanistan. The International Security Assistance Force (ISAF) was created under a United Nations mandate. In time, NATO took over the coordination of ISAF troops across the country.

Canadian forces had started out in the south of Afghanistan at the Kandahar Airfield. The second major stage of the Canadian military campaign, Operation Athena, was centred at Camp Julien in Kabul. Roughly two thousand troops assembled at Camp Julien at the height of Operation Athena, which was a peace support mission, a NATO term with a definition similar to that of a peacekeeping mission, but with a different legal framework.

By the spring of 2005, the Liberal government had launched the third stage of Canada's involvement in Afghanistan—the creation of a provincial reconstruction team. Operations at Camp Julien began to wind down and by the fall of 2005, 250 troops were settled in the PRT, which was eventually backed by a battle group of roughly one thousand soldiers deployed elsewhere in the south.

The move away from the relative quiet of Kabul and toward the heartland of the Taliban marked a significant change for Canadian troops. Throughout 2006, the situation became increasingly dangerous, with a spike in deaths and injuries due to suicide bomb attacks, IEDs, and combat. In May, Stephen Harper's new government proposed an extension of Canada's mission in Afghanistan—this time until 2009. Members of Parliament narrowly passed the motion in a 149 to 145 vote in the House of Commons. According to one estimate, Canadians will spend four billion dollars on the Afghanistan mission by 2009.

Across Canada, public support for the mission rises and falls with the news of the war. A series of polls conducted for the Canadian Broadcasting Corporation by Environics suggested that while Canadians approved of the country's role in the early years of the effort, public enthusiasm has dwindled over time. In 2002 some three-quarters of Canadians supported Canada's involvement. By the spring of 2006, support for the mission had dropped to fewer than 50 per cent of those polled.

From the beginning, Canadians were at the very least ambivalent and most certainly confused by what was happening in Afghanistan. An Environics poll in November 2006 reported that 24 per cent of those interviewed thought Canadians were performing peacekeeping duties in Afghanistan; 22 per cent thought the soldiers were there to support US troops and US foreign policy. Eighteen per cent said they believed Canadians were offering humanitarian assistance and reconstruction. That public confusion registered with troops overseas; Paul had taped colourful handmade cards into his diary, sent to him from Alberta schoolchildren in late 2005. The cards read "Merry Christmas Peacekeepers."

Although Canada's mission in Afghanistan did not fit the traditional Canadian notion of peacekeeping, the public could be forgiven for misunderstanding the reality. There had been no public debate in 2001 when the Canadian government decided to send troops to Afghanistan to work with the American military. As the Canadian mission changed shape, moving from a "stabilization" effort in the beginning, to a peace support mission, to a full-out combat role led by the Americans outside of the NATO umbrella in the early part of 2006, the public had to pay close attention to keep up. Canadians were still stinging with the shame of soldier misconduct in the Somalia affair, and perplexed about the role of Canadian peacekeepers in the Balkans in the 1990s. They were justified in wondering what had ever happened to the tidy vision of the Canadian in the blue beret, making the world a more peaceful and hopeful place.

For Paul Franklin, the mission's goal of defense, development, and diplomacy was crystal clear. By September 2005, he and his fellow soldiers at the PRT were assigned to provide security and support for the parliamentary elections. Although the elections were peaceful and considered a success—12.6 million Afghans registered to vote out of a population of 21.7 million—by the late fall, the positive news was muted to say the least.

During the election, there had been few insurgent assaults or interruptions to the proceedings. Within a few months, the attacks by al Qaeda and Taliban fighters were on the rise and Canadians were in the crosshairs time after time. In October a rocket blast struck the Canadian Embassy in Kabul. In November and December, Canadian convoys were repeatedly attacked and soldiers were hurt.

During this period, Paul said Canadian troops grew increasingly nervous. He noted in his diary on December 4 that his friend Jason was involved in a suicide attack while on the way back from a village medical outreach clinic. Two Canadian trucks were hit, but not much damage was done. Though Jason was covered in blood and bits of tissue from the suicide bomber, he wasn't hurt.

Paul liked to tease Jason about his close call, but the incidents set soldiers at the PRT on edge. Paul's two-week Christmas leave was coming up soon and he was looking forward to it. "Let's hope nothing else happens," Paul wrote in his diary. As he penned the words, he never dreamed he would soon be at the centre of his own news story.

Back in Canada, Audra, too, heard the reports of escalating attacks in the south of Afghanistan, but she remained confident her husband would be safe.

"I know the risks. I'm fully aware of what he does. I just had a lot of faith that he was a well-trained soldier. He was with some good guys and I knew that he would come home and be fine. It never occurred to me that he would get hurt. That is the last thing I thought would happen."

Glyn Berry's death and the injuries of Paul and his buddies Jeff and Will marked the beginning of a frightening time for Canadians at home and in Afghanistan.

Paul (kneeling on right) poses with his comrades in B Company, 4 Platoon, 3 Section, 3rd Battalion, Princess Patricia's Canadian Light Infantry, in November 2005. Kneeling on the left is Cpl. Jeff Bailey. Pte. Will Salikin stands third from the left.

Photo credit: Reproduced courtesy of the Department of National Defence and with the permission of the Minister of Public Works and Government Services, 2007

In 2006 thirty-six Canadian soldiers died, bringing the total number of Canadian deaths in Afghanistan to forty-four. One of the dead soldiers was Capt. Nichola Goddard, the first Canadian woman killed in a combat role. Five years into the mission, 194 Canadian soldiers had been injured.

By the end of 2006, roughly ten thousand Canadian soldiers had served in Afghanistan. Paul Franklin's war came home with him.

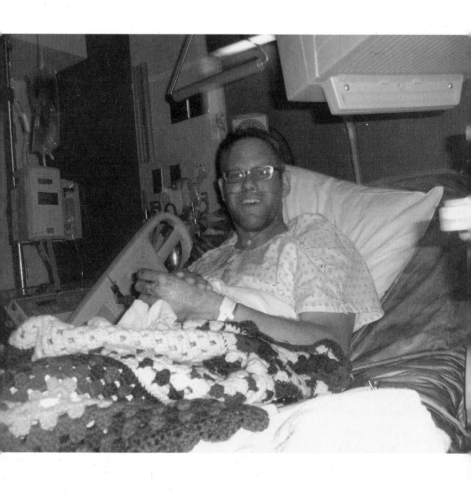

6

TIME TO DECIDE

PAUL WAS IN THE OPERATING ROOM, drifting on a sea of anesthetic. Dr. James Wagg, an orthopedic surgeon at the University of Alberta hospital and a major in the Canadian military, snapped on his surgical gloves and walked into the steel and tile of the operating room for a first, up-close glimpse at his new patient. Though James wasn't scheduled to be covering the OR that day, he was anxious to assess the damage inflicted on Paul by the suicide car bomb in Kandahar. It wasn't pretty, but then most blast injuries are not.

Several factors make an explosive blast one of the most dangerous wounds in war. Shrapnel created by the eruption of a rocket-propelled grenade, a suicide bomb, or a land mine pierces whatever gets in its way like a red-hot arrow and sends shock waves through body tissues, even those that haven't been destroyed by the explosion itself. The shocked tissue at first may appear pink and healthy, but it can be so traumatized that it soon dies and then rots.

Complicating the actual blast injury is a bit of science that goes hand in hand with an explosive force. Even as the blast pushes energy outwards, ripping flesh from bone, a vacuum is created, which sucks material inward. Dust, dirt, gravel, and feces—whatever happens to be lying around, including the shattered bones of a suicide bomber or a shard of bulletproof glass, may become imbedded deep in a blast wound. This can lead to an infection as potentially deadly as the wound itself.

Months after his injury, when an oozing sore on the stump of one leg was particularly slow to heal, Paul found himself engaged in a grisly mental fantasy as he gently probed the exterior of the wound. Was a scrap of his assailant's body, perhaps a fragment of tooth, trapped inside Paul's body and trying to get out?

In fact, during the first operation performed on Paul at the University of Alberta hospital, a debridement, the surgeon found bits of rubber, likely from the exploding tires of the G-Wagon, buried deep inside the wound.

This was the first of six surgical debridements Paul would undergo at the U of A hospital, in addition to several he had already endured at Landstuhl. Blast wounds are typically left open and packed with sterile absorbent material for a period of time to allow easy access for ongoing cleaning and scraping away of dead tissue. Closing the wound before the tissue is healthy and on the mend increases the risk of infection. Dead tissue has no blood supply, no way to deliver bug-busting white blood cells to the site, so infection can run rampant. Debridement can sometimes be done on the ward without anesthetic. But in Paul's case, the pain would have been unbearable, so he was wheeled to the OR and put under for each procedure.

"In terms of limb injury, it ranks up there as some of the worst I've seen," James said, remembering his initial surgical assessment of Paul. "His left leg was completely blown off and it doesn't get worse than that."

But the right leg gave the surgeon more reason to hope. While it was missing hunks of the calf, a lot could be done to fix that. The wound vacuum was doing its job by sucking body fluids through a custom-cut sponge in the calf and bringing the edges of the wound together. An external fixator also supported the damaged leg with pins that went through the skin into the bone. The fixator, which is like a metal frame, is used temporarily until surgery can create a permanent repair. In some cases, it can stay on the patient for months at a time while the bones heal; some fixators are strong enough to support a patient's weight while he or she learns to walk again.

Although Paul's right leg may have looked beyond repair to the untrained eye, to an orthopedic surgeon, it wasn't half bad. The limb still had relatively normal neurological function. Paul could move his toes and had good pulses in his foot. He was slightly feverish, so there was clearly some infection. Still, James felt positive about the prospects for saving the right leg. He ordered some tests, including an angiogram to look at the arteries to see if they were healthy enough to sustain a long period of reconstruction. James believed that trying to save the right leg was the way to ensure Paul the best recovery possible.

Having one leg would be an enormous advantage for Paul. It is much easier to learn to walk on one prosthetic leg if you've still got one leg of your own. The real leg provides balance, support, and sheer muscle power. A foot connects the body to the ground and transmits sensory information about whether the surface below is bumpy, slippery, or steep. Indeed, as Paul would hear over and over again to his eternal rancour, few people who have both legs amputated above the knee—known as a bilateral transfemoral in medical jargon—ever walk again. The vast majority must accept life in a wheelchair.

Often that's because bilateral amputees are older people—diabetics or people with vascular disease whose amputations stem from declining circulation. Older people don't have the strength to heave themselves around on two artificial legs. According to Edmonton rehabilitation specialist Dr. Jackie Hebert, a double, above-the-knee amputee uses 200 to 300 per cent more energy to walk on prostheses than a normal person uses to walk on real legs. Even for young people, like the American veterans in their twenties who lost limbs in the war in Iraq, such an amputation was a daunting prospect. Jackie, who consulted with Paul in those early days, had only heard of a couple of people in North America with the same degree of injury who had ever walked on prostheses. The muscle capability, the aerobic endurance, and the sheer willpower required had defeated all but the most exceptional characters.

>>>

AFTER THAT FIRST SURGERY, HOSPITAL STAFF wheeled Paul back to 3F2, the sixteen-bed trauma unit that would be his home for six weeks. If patients hover between life and death, intensive care is the only choice. But when they can breathe on their own, they head to 3F2, which not only offers expert physical care, but intense psychological support for people whose injuries have dramatically changed their lives. These patients may have been in car accidents or industrial mishaps, but their experiences have a common thread: their bodies have been inexorably altered and their minds and spirits need help with the transition.

When Paul arrived at the U of A hospital to begin his recovery, he stayed on 3F2, and not just because of the severity of his wounds. 3F2 also has an arrangement with the Canadian military. A number of military nurses and doctors hone their skills on this unit so that they are prepared to offer patients the best treatment possible when they are shipped out to the theatre of war.

Within a week of Paul arriving at the hospital, Audra had established a visiting routine. She dropped Simon at school. Then she drove directly to the hospital, praying for a parking spot somewhere close to the sprawling structure, located on the University of Alberta campus. Boom-time construction projects stacked toward the sky and snarled traffic in the area. Audra liked to have breakfast with Paul before the parade of family, friends, and military officials began. She picked up some yoghurt and fresh fruit in the main-floor cafeteria and squeezed into the elevator. Exiting at the third floor, Audra walked across the bright pedway that connected the elevators to the trauma unit. The sunny atrium below was brimming with plants, and it gave Audra a lift to see the touch of green. Outside, the world was white with snow. It felt like it had already been a long winter.

From down the hall, Audra saw hospital staff moving in and out of Paul's room, number 16, which was located directly across from the nursing station. They must be changing his dressings, she said to herself. She decided to stop in at the nursing station to chat with nurse Cheryl Feniak, unit manager of 3F2. From the moment they had met, Audra liked Cheryl, a blonde woman with long, curly hair whose cheerful pragmatism appealed to Audra's no-nonsense personality. Like Audra, Cheryl was the kind of woman who gave you her full attention when it was needed, but she was not one to mince words.

Are you guys doing pizza night on Friday?

Audra smiled and nodded yes.

To assure the Franklin family some privacy, Cheryl had helped them revive a Friday night tradition of ordering in pizza. Cheryl would post a No Visitors note on the door, just to give Paul, Audra, and Simon a chance to snuggle on the hospital bed and take a break from the relentless stream of well-meaning guests.

Leaving Cheryl, Audra grabbed a gown from the metal rack in the hallway and prepared to enter Paul's room. Paul was in isolation, having picked up two multi-drug-resistant bacteria in Afghanistan. If visitors were going from Paul's room to visit Jeff or Will, who were at the same hospital, they had to wear gloves. Otherwise, just a gown would do.

Paul and Audra had quickly become accustomed to the ongoing attention of a multitude of well-wishers—everyone from Brig.-Gen. Tim Grant, head of Land Forces Western Area, to Cmdre. Margaret Kavanagh, the head of the Canadian Forces health services group. Friends and family members, including Paul's twin sister Nancy from Toronto, had come from out of town. Paul's parents, Ron and Barb, and his older sister, Janice, made regular trips from their home in Calgary. Faye and Simon were up nearly every day. Countless officers and enlisted men and women in camouflage gear made appearances throughout the morning and afternoon. One of Paul's closest non-military friends, Andrew Appleton, had come to town from Vancouver to help Audra for six weeks and was often pulling bedside duty. Even members of the public who did not know Paul at all found their way up to room 16.

Some of the nurses on 3F2 joked that it was like having a movie star on the ward. Ever since Paul arrived, he had been the focus of intense scrutiny by the media nationwide and the military brass, not to mention ordinary folk who perceived him as a war hero. The attention was linked, in part, to the death of Glyn Berry, the first Canadian diplomat to be killed in the line of duty in nearly half a century. (A Canadian diplomat had died in Egypt in 1954 and two were killed in Vietnam in the mid-1950s.) Paul, Will, and Jeff were also among the most seriously injured soldiers to return home since Canada had entered the war in Afghanistan in 2001. Add the fact that Paul and his wounded comrades were part of Canada's first military combat mission in more than fifty years and it meant big news.

Canadian media coverage had also shifted since the Korean War. The media's appetite for news stories was voracious, with intense competition among twenty-four-hour television news channels, newspapers, radio, and the Internet. Every newscast required a fresh meal, and reporters were foraging, each new angle a tidbit to be digested at the top of the hour. With more than thirteen thousand regular force soldiers, reservists, civilian staff, and family members stationed at Canadian Forces Base Edmonton, the military was a top story in the prairie city.

From the earliest days of Canada's involvement in the international campaign against terrorism in Afghanistan, Edmonton's soldiers were front-page news across the country. In February 2002, the city's own 3rd Battalion, Princess Patricia's Canadian Light Infantry battle group, became the first Canadian unit assigned to a combat operation since Korea. The first Canadian soldiers killed in Afghanistan were also from Edmonton. Sgt. Marc Leger, Cpl. Ainsworth Dyer, Pte. Richard Green, and Pte. Nathan Smith died when a US fighter jet dropped a 250-kilogram bomb on a Canadian live-fire night exercise near Kandahar in April 2002. Their deaths rocked the local community and reverberated nationwide. When Glyn Berry died and three Edmonton soldiers were gravely injured in January 2006, the military's profile in Edmonton and across Canada shot up once again.

Other factors pushed Paul to the forefront. He had never been a naturally outgoing person—his mother says he dropped out of a class in public speaking at college because he was not the kind to draw attention to himself—but something changed after the injury. Paul embraced a new and very public role: to make sure the Canadian people understood what it was like to be a Canadian soldier serving in Afghanistan.

"It's not just my story," he would say, over and over again, in media interviews, or while talking with strangers who swarmed around him at Costco. Many soldiers had been wounded, and some killed. Families were struggling to rebuild their lives. Partners and parents were learning that war changes people, sometimes permanently, and these changes might not be welcome.

Handsome and with a self-deprecating sense of humour, Paul was a natural with the media from the day of his first press conference at

Paul and Audra host a press conference at the University of Alberta Hospital in February 2006.

Photo credit: Rick MacWilliam

the University of Alberta Hospital. There, he brought out the good luck charm from his G-Wagon, Jenna the hula dancer, instinctively aware that the media like props. He joked and laughed with reporters, remarking that while he and Audra had become closer since the incident, he wouldn't recommend a near-death experience as a way to buff up your marriage.

From the start, Audra had also made herself available to the press, because she was determined that the public would see the best possible face of the military family. Well-spoken and media savvy, Audra was not intimidated by the scrum of reporters and flashing cameras that gathered at her home within hours of the announcement of the suicide bombing. This was her chance to show Canadians that military families were tough and resilient, and they supported the soldiers and the mission. Yet there was never any artifice about Audra. She didn't push the stiff upper lip. From the start, she acknowledged the painful struggle that gripped her family. Her son was traumatized, her husband was reeling, she was suffering from migraine headaches and panic attacks, and she made no bones about it. They carried on.

There was another reason the Franklins decided to go public. Jeff and Will were in worse shape than Paul, having suffered severe head injuries. Their futures were uncertain; there was a chance Jeff wouldn't survive his ordeal. Audra knew the last thing those soldiers' families needed was to endure the media hordes. The Franklins were their shield.

All these factors combined to keep the spotlight on the Franklin family, turning each day into a blur of activity, decision-making, and new-found fame. Paul and Audra were rarely alone. In some ways, that was okay. Paul seemed galvanized by the attention. For Audra it was a distraction. Being alone, just the two of them, was hard.

>>>

IT WAS GETTING CLOSE TO VALENTINE'S DAY. Audra passed the hospital gift shop, festooned with shiny red helium balloons and lacy boxes of candy, and remembered that she had to get Valentine cards for Simon to give out at school. That thought flew from her mind when she entered room 16. James was there and the doctor had some news for the couple.

Audra walked toward the bed, where Paul sat upright. He had tried to decorate the room to make it seem less sterile. There was a hand-woven camel hair rug from Afghanistan thrown over one chair, and a red, yellow, and orange quilt at the end of the bed. One of Simon's GI Joes sat on the bedside table, as well as a miniature G-Wagon, which Paul used to show visitors how his vehicle had blown up.

Paul motioned Audra to come closer, giving her the usual bright grin and quick kiss. She could see that today, as with many days, there was a lot going on behind Paul's smile.

Dr. Wagg thinks they can save my leg, Paul said.

James launched into his explanation. The angiogram, a dye test, revealed that two of three arteries offered a good blood supply to the injured right leg, and this was critical for healing. After consulting with plastic surgeons and the seven other orthopedic surgeons on Paul's care team, James told the couple the medical consensus was positive: there was a good chance the leg could be rehabilitated.

The plan was to take muscles from Paul's back to replace the missing calf tissue. The bone between the knee and ankle that was also largely absent would be replaced through something called bone transport. Bone transport involves cutting a healthy bit of bone and attaching it to a frame with tiny cranks on it. As the healthy bone regenerates, the crank slowly pulls the new bone down until it can be attached to the ankle. Skin grafted from the upper thigh would cover the reconstructed calf. All the while, Paul's leg would be pinned into a walkable external fixator for up to a year to allow healing to be completed.

Paul looked at the surgeon and asked the first question.

How do you know it will be successful?

James said there was no guarantee. The orthopedic team thought there was a reasonably good chance the right leg would heal.

If you still had one good leg, James said to Paul, we might not be so aggressive in suggesting this course of treatment. But you've already lost one leg. If we can save your second leg, you've got a much better chance of learning to walk again on a prosthesis.

The room was silent. James took that as his signal to move on. Audra looked right into Paul's eyes. She knew it was up to her husband to decide what to do. At the same time, both she and her mother had earlier expressed their opinion that keeping the leg might be the best approach. Faye prayed to her dead husband, Bill, to send a sign to Paul to keep the leg.

Paul turned to Audra. How is Simon this morning? Did he get his math test back?

>>>

THE MIDDLE OF THE NIGHT CAN be quiet on 3F2. Nurse Jenn Anderson often used the downtime to catch up on patient charts. The last couple of nights, she'd been spending time with Paul, because he couldn't sleep and needed to talk.

Paul was one of her favourite patients, the kind nurses will try and do a little bit extra for when they can. Sometimes that meant bringing him a warmed blanket, or some juice with ice in it. He never requested these things; Paul was the perfect patient, doing exactly what he needed to do to get better, including religiously applying antibiotic ointment to his hands and exercising his fingers so he would heal better and avoid plastic surgery. Cheerful and chatty, Paul did not complain, even on his hardest, most painful days. So when he asked Jenn to stop by his room later in the night, if she had time, Jenn knew something was up.

I don't know what to do, Paul began. The nurse pulled up a chair in the dimly lit room and sat down. She crossed her legs and rested her chin in her hand.

Dr. Wagg says he thinks they can save my right leg, and it would be better for the future, for helping me walk, but I have such a bad feeling about this leg, Paul said.

Why is that? Jenn waited for his reply.

Paul still battled an infection in his right leg from the initial injury and he had a gut feeling it wasn't going to get better. There was still the chance a system-wide infection could prove life-threatening, and Paul didn't want to take more risks with his health. He had seen bad infections as a medic and believed if he let things go on, he might suffer greater losses, perhaps even his life. The doctors said this was highly unlikely, but Paul didn't believe them.

I know my own body, Paul said. And this just doesn't feel right.

He worried that if he opted to save the leg and it didn't work, a year and a half would have passed and he'd be back where he started. No, actually, it would be worse, because he would be missing major muscles in his back.

And then I'll be in a wheelchair without enough strength to push myself around, Paul said.

The combination of the length of time needed for healing and the uncertain outcome made him nervous. If doctors amputated right away, he could heal within a month and be ready to get on a pair of prosthetic limbs shortly thereafter. On the other hand, if the reconstruction of his right leg worked, Paul would be sure to stand tall once again.

Jenn could only offer a sympathetic ear. She hoped that was enough.

>>>

IN THE END, PAUL TOLD JAMES he wanted the right leg to come off. James wavered between wanting to respect his patient's right to make his own decision and a deep concern that Paul was making the choice for all the wrong reasons. James knew that after a traumatic injury, some patients could end up feeling angry or hostile about a broken body part, or simply detached from it. He worried Paul associated his injured right leg with the incident in Afghanistan, linking it with the death of Glyn Berry and the sorry shape of his military buddies. It was as if Paul was somehow offended the leg was still hanging around, making his life more complicated and his choices more difficult. James asked Paul if he might consider talking with a psychiatrist to explore the way he felt about the right leg.

"No, Doc, it's not that," Paul said. "I just don't think that leg is ever going to be of any use to me. And the sooner I deal with that, the sooner I can get out of here and get on with my life. It's time I was home. I really need to get home."

On Valentine's Day, surgeons amputated Paul's right leg. At first, doctors took it off just below the knee, hoping to salvage the bending joint, so valuable when it comes to fitting a prosthesis. However, within a few days, Paul had a fever; another infection had developed. On February 21, surgeons went in again and got rid of the knee, wrapping most of Paul's thigh muscles around the bottom of the thigh bone to make a cushion for the stump. It was over.

On 3F2, doctors and nurses alike marvelled at Paul's attitude. Even on days when Paul felt like crap, he greeted James with a bright "What's up, what are we doing today, Doc?" Nurse Julie Kosterman recalls that she was impressed that Paul was neither bitter nor angry with the suicide bomber who had changed his life. He could see the world from the bomber's perspective.

"Why would I have to go to Afghanistan and invade their country? That's what they think," Paul said. "I'm the enemy and the bad guy, even though from our perspective, we're trying to give them a new lease on life. But from their perspective, we're not."

Paul told Julie the suicide bomber was just a soldier doing his job, and he couldn't be mad at a soldier doing his job. Paul even claimed to respect the attacker for the skill it took to be able to hit Paul's vehicle with such precision.

Julie asked Paul if helping the people in Afghanistan was worth losing his legs. He told her it was.

>>>

CHERYL FENIAK HAD SEEN A FEW injured soldiers come through 3F2 before Paul arrived, and she has seen quite a few since. She has never met another soldier like Paul. He was the man who didn't grieve. If Paul were angry, staff didn't know it. If the man had a bad day, he didn't show it. Health care workers said military patients often had a "let's get on with it" approach to healing, perhaps created by their military training, with its focus on getting the job done. Even among military people, Paul was unusual. Always upbeat, always offering a grin to visitors and staff, Paul was determined not to let his injury win.

"It sticks out like a sore thumb," Cheryl later said of Paul's approach to his recovery. "I've spent nearly twenty-five years working with neuro-trauma populations, and you don't see this but maybe once. If you know anything about loss and grieving, whether you lose a person or lose a part of yourself, you go through the grieving process. With Paul, I never saw that. I was waiting for him to have the moment when he crashed. But I never saw that with him."

For a man who left the world of sales because he hated always having to be "on," Paul had accepted a new role—that of the recovering soldier—which left him few unguarded moments, and few opportunities to let his cheerful determination flag. As he prepared to move from the acute care hospital to the rehabilitation hospital across town, Cheryl wondered how long he could go on like that.

"I'm not sold," she said.

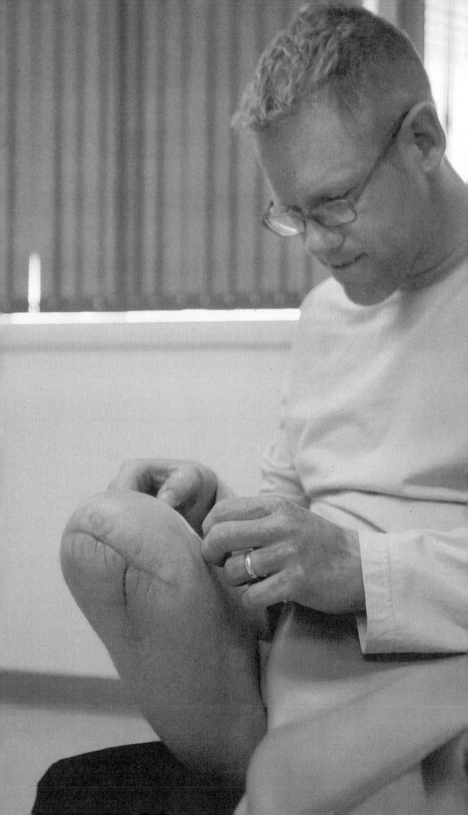

7

THE NEW NORMAL

PAUL SAT UP IN HIS BED at the Glenrose Rehabilitation Hospital and looked down at his stumps. Some medical professionals use the phrase residual limb, or the even more arcane term residuûm, when they refer to an amputated leg. Bev Agur, Paul's new physiotherapist at the Glenrose, simply called them legs, even though they ended at mid-thigh. Paul wasn't one to fear words; he didn't mind calling them stumps. It wasn't a pretty word, but it was accurate. Like a tree stump, his legs were a fraction of what they used to be. Like a tree stump, Paul's legs were rooted, not in the ground, but in a powerful psyche, Paul's biggest asset as he began his recovery.

Thicker from the hip and rump, where his gluteal muscles still offered power and bulk, Paul's stumps each narrowed as they traveled down the thigh, coming to a softly rounded end that looked like the stitched seam of a misshapen football. Audra noted in a thoughtful voice that the stitches at the bottom of each stump reminded her of a smiley face with teeth. Bev said lots of amputees, especially early on, couldn't look at their maimed limbs. Paul had no problem with that. Although he couldn't put weight on the stumps—they would always need a socket to move him anywhere—he was grateful the stumps were as long as they were, twenty-eight centimetres from his

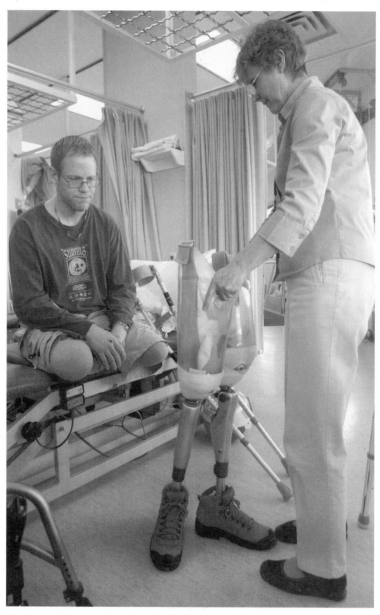

Physiotherapist Bev Agur holds up Paul's new artificial legs during a physiotherapy session at the Glenrose Rehabilitation Hospital.

Photo credit: Bruce Edwards

hip bones. Any shorter, and it would have been much more difficult to support a set of prosthetic legs. As it was, Glenrose prosthetist Mike Stobbe was breezily confident two new legs could be fitted for Paul's stumps.

Of course, fitting them was one thing. Walking on them was quite another. For weeks now, medical professionals had been delivering Paul the hard facts; odds were that Paul would not walk again after suffering a double, above-the-knee amputation.

"That's their stock answer," he noted wryly when confronted with the doctor's pronouncements, which were based on their own experience with amputees and the medical literature. "You'll never walk again. Next."

Paul refused to accept that he would be spending most of his time in a wheelchair. In the weeks after the explosion, he had experienced that way of living and he didn't much like it. For one thing, people talk to those in wheelchairs in a louder voice, as if not being able to walk means you are also deaf, or stupid.

"In a wheelchair, people ignore you completely or cater to you horribly," Paul said. "It's a funky, funky experience."

Still, amputees pay a price to stand tall. One of the many problems with walking on prostheses is that it requires a huge amount of metabolic energy. It is vastly more energy efficient, and faster, to use a wheelchair than to walk on prosthetic legs, which weigh about 4.5 kilograms each. Wheelchairs are more stable, and quite easy to maneuver with practice. Moving in a wheelchair leaves the hands free; wearing prostheses requires the use of arm crutches, at least at first, so carrying something or shaking hands becomes a big deal. Paul considered these trade-offs as he prepared his body for a challenge that made climbing a mountain or pounding through a triathalon seem like a warm-up.

He faced huge obstacles to standing up. It would have been an enormous bonus if Paul had been able to keep his knee when his right leg was amputated. Below-the-knee amputees still have that wondrous bumpy joint that allows them the luxury of raising and lowering the body. Oh, for a knee. Even one.

There was a knock at Paul's door. Bev poked her masked face into the room. Sorry about all this stuff, she said as she pulled up a chair, motioning to the gloves and gown she wore in addition to the blue surgical mask.

For the first week Paul was at the Glenrose, the only dedicated rehabilitation hospital serving Northern Alberta and the Canadian north, he was in isolation. He still carried two forms of multi-drug-resistant bacteria picked up in Afghanistan and was a risk to patients with weak immune systems, even though he was symptom-free. Until staff got the infection-control protocol figured out, Paul would have to spend a lot of time in his room. Bev and Mike came to see him there to get started on the rehab plan.

In some ways, it wasn't a bad thing to begin physiotherapy on a small scale, in Paul's room. Paul was "deconditioned" in physiotherapy terms, which meant he was still exhausted and had lost muscle tone and aerobic strength in the nearly two months he'd been on bed rest. So Bev started with simple exercises. Patients who lose their legs also lose a sense of where their body rests in space, and their centre of gravity changes. Bev began to work on restoring basic balance by tossing Paul a ball while he sat up in bed, with more and more force, so he could learn to stabilize himself in his new body. There was a trapeze over Paul's bed. He began to do chin-ups and other arm strengthening exercises. Bev also gave Paul five-pound-weights and big rubber bands to use for resistance training for his arms.

To Paul, these felt like discouragingly puny efforts. He thought of his last big endurance test, a marathon in Dubai that he had enjoyed while on his way back to Afghanistan after his holiday in California. Now that was hard work. This stuff was for babies. Still, he knew

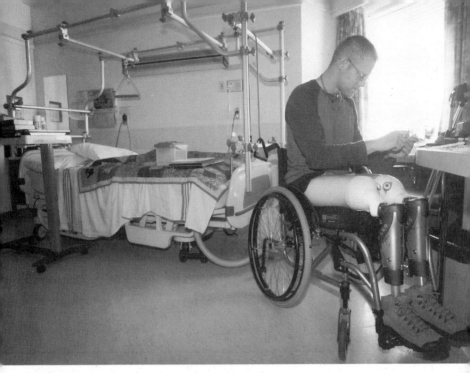

Paul has some down time in his room at the Glenrose.

Photo credit: Bruce Edwards

that's where he had to start. His body was clumsy, tired, and scarred. It reminded him every single day of his new reality, and how far he had to go to become, as he constantly repeated, "the man I was."

"You always want to recover what you've lost. To be who you were is always something you want when you're going through something like this," Paul said. "Except that person doesn't exist anymore. I have to discover the new me, what we call the new normal. I don't think of it as a frightening thing; I think of it just as a challenge, a very long-off challenge, and it's tiring because it's not going quick enough for me even though I'm doing really well. I'm not fast enough."

As Paul uttered those words, he had no clue what the new normal would be.

Before she wrapped up the modified physio session in Paul's room, Bev gave him some balls of different sizes so he could toss them around later that evening when Simon arrived. This would give the boy something to do when he came to visit and would give Paul another opportunity for exercise. Great, thought Paul. Tossing a ball to your dad as he sits in bed in a hospital filled with old people on walkers and young people in wheelchairs. That sounds like fun.

Bev didn't know it at the time, but suggesting Paul play ball with Simon went to the core of one of Paul's biggest fears. Paul was always the "cool" dad on the block, the one who learned to skateboard just so he could play with Simon and the neighbourhood kids. To Paul, being a good dad meant riding bikes with Simon and kicking a soccer ball in the backyard. A man who could not play sports or roughhouse with his son was a poor excuse for a father. Paul was jealous when he saw Darren and Simon together. Whenever they met, Simon would fling himself at his older friend, and the two would have a good wrestle.

Paul genuinely feared he would have nothing in common with Simon as he grew up, and would lose a relationship that meant more to him than he had ever known. He wondered what Simon would remember about his father as he grew older. Would Simon ever remember a time when his dad had legs?

>>>

PAUL WHEELED DOWN TO THE GLENROSE gym for physiotherapy treatment one week after he arrived at the rehab hospital. He looked around the big, bright room, fitted out with a number of broad, vinyl-covered beds. There were two sets of parallel bars and a variety of steps of different depths for learning how to climb. Around the perimeter of the gym was a collection of walkers and crutches. Curtains hung between some of the beds for those who needed privacy.

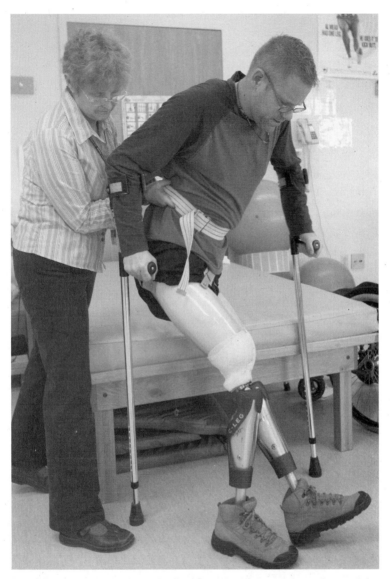

Bev holds onto a strap around Paul's waist as he learns to get up from a sitting position with his new legs.

Photo credit: Bruce Edwards

Paul started each of his two daily sessions with a warm-up. Rolling to one side on the bed, he stretched his right stump, which ached from his exercise efforts. Leaning over Paul, Bev used a protractor-like device to chart her patient's range of motion, moving his leg to the outside, then as far back as possible, on both right and left sides. Paul had to stretch the few muscles he had left in his legs as long and hard as he possibly could in order to coax the maximum amount of motion from them. He needed every ounce of pull that every muscle fibre in his stumps could provide. In just a few days, Paul would be getting his new legs. That's when the real battle would begin.

Paul had learned some of the basics at the University of Alberta Hospital, such as moving from his bed into a wheelchair, and from a wheelchair onto a toilet seat. He could get in and out of the car with relative ease. These movements are known as level transfers. Next, Paul had to learn to move between surfaces of different heights. His first goal was to get a weekend pass to go home. He and Audra had purchased a new house with a full set of stairs to the second floor, but the lift to the second floor would not be installed for two more months. In the meantime, Paul had to learn to "bum" up and down the stairs. Like a toddler learning to negotiate steps for the first time, he had to heave himself up and lower himself down the steps on his bottom. Bev had to make sure he was capable of this activity before she let him go home on a weekend pass. By March 17, the end of his second week at the Glenrose, Paul had mastered the skill.

Bev scheduled Paul's physio sessions when the gym was relatively quiet so he wouldn't be exposed to as many other patients. After every hour-long session, she wiped down the vinyl beds and separated Paul's equipment in a special bin to avoid spreading the Afghanistan bacteria.

Bev was nervous, and not just about infection control. The military had initially told Paul he could do his rehabilitation at

Walter Reed Army Medical Center in Washington, DC, a world-famous facility that had worked with thousands of American veterans hurt in Iraq. Paul had turned down that chance, partly because he wanted to be close to friends and family as he recovered, but also because he believed it was important for Canadian specialists to develop more expertise in war-related amputations. Paul wouldn't be the last Canadian soldier to lose limbs to a devastating explosion.

Bev knew Paul had been offered the first-class ticket, and she hoped he wouldn't regret saying no. A small woman in her mid-fifties with short, curly brown hair and wire-rimmed glasses, Bev had been a physiotherapist for more than thirty years. In all those years, she had never treated a bilateral, above-the-knee amputee who intended to walk on prostheses. Though friendly and engaging, Paul was an intimidating character. Bev had already watched him on the news numerous times, and could see that he was not frightened by the media or reluctant to speak his own mind.

Bev knew Paul had high expectations for his recovery, and she was worried. Would she able to help him reach his potential? Certainly she had a good team to work with. Mike was responsible for fitting and fiddling with the prostheses and making sure they did what they were designed to do. Rehabilitation expert Jackie Hebert, Paul's doctor at the Glenrose, was in charge of the big-picture stuff, like how to deal with phantom limb pain and determining how the relatively fresh wound on Paul's right leg was healing. The big question—how do we get this guy up off the floor?—was Bev's responsibility, and she knew it.

Paul had strengths working in his favour. He could count on the emotional support of a strong group of friends and family members, as well as the financial and moral support of the Canadian military. Gen. Rick Hillier kept in regular contact with Paul. Other military and political leaders, including two prime ministers—Paul Martin and Stephen Harper—had passed on their best wishes. The military

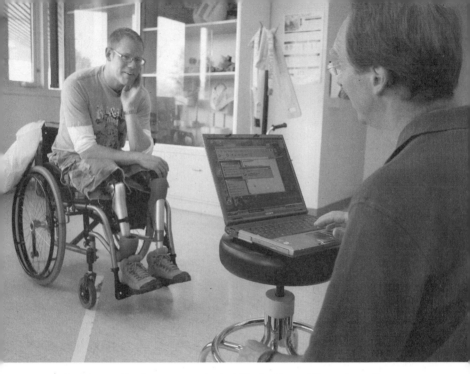

Paul chats with Glenrose prosthetist Mike Stobbe as Mike makes adjustments to Paul's C-legs.

Photo credit: Bruce Edwards

paid for any medical aids required. If Paul needed a special device, or a different kind of wheelchair, he got it. Paul also had a strong body to work with. He was young and fit and determined.

"He had good arm strength, so he could lift his body weight no problem," Bev said. "It would have been much harder if he hadn't been in such great shape to start."

Daily at the Glenrose, Paul pushed his own fitness a little further. He could feel the ropey strength in his abdominal muscles returning with every set of crunches. When he thought he couldn't do another push-up, Paul squeezed out five more. Bev told him his hip and trunk muscles needed to be stronger to do the work his legs used to do. She taught him specific exercises. Paul tackled them vigorously.

Most of Paul's thigh muscles—quadriceps and hamstrings—had been cut during the amputations, but Paul did have some muscles available for the hard work ahead. These were the muscles found in Paul's bum area, the gluteus maximus (gluts in gym talk) and the iliopsoas, or hip flexors, as well as two muscle groups on the inside and outside of each thigh, known respectively as the adductors and the abductors. Bev developed a special regime for strengthening the muscles that would be responsible for lifting the prostheses up, propelling them forward and keeping Paul steady so he wouldn't fall over.

In another corner of the Glenrose, a compassionate craftsman was creating a custom-designed set of new legs for Paul. Mike Stobbe is a tall, slim man with a bushy moustache. A dedicated prosthetist, he began to shape the first of two different models that the soldier would try out in the weeks ahead. The ultimate in prosthetic knee units was the C-Leg, a thirty-eight-thousand dollar limb with the most advanced technology available, but the legs had to be ordered from Germany and that took time. Mike fitted Paul for a simpler pair of knee units, just to get him started.

Before he could fit the sockets of the prosthetic legs, he had to wait until both of Paul's stumps had completely healed and some of the post-operative swelling had gone down. Then Paul began wearing gel liners—long, flesh-coloured socks with a slightly rubbery lining. The liners helped shape the legs so they would fit snugly in the prosthetic sockets. Many amputees find the liners more comfortable than sitting around with a bare leg, and Paul was one of them. Even after his wounds healed, Paul frequently had leg pain. Phantom limb pain occurs after an amputation when the nerves, disorganized and confused about having no limbs to work with, fire randomly. Paul endured pain that he could have sworn was coming from his mangled right leg, even though it was no longer there. Occasionally, he longed to scratch a fiery itch on his foot. Gel liners seemed to rein in the hapless nerves. They also helped Paul adjust to the feeling of constant compression on his stumps, something he would need in order to walk on prosthetic legs.

Mike designed the prosthetic sockets by taking a digital image of each of Paul's legs with something called a T-ring, a metal circle with eight cameras on it. A black and white striped sock went over the amputated limb. Mike positioned the T-ring around it. Then cameras snapped numerous digital photographs. The lines on the sock created a digital image that came up on Mike's laptop computer. Mike sent that image off to a prosthetic carver, which made a solid model of the socket, called a positive image. That was delivered back to the Glenrose hospital's prosthetic lab, which looks like an artist's studio, complete with white plaster sculptures of limbs drying here and there. There, a prosthetic technician draped a special flexible plastic over the socket. When solidified, it formed a negative image—a hollow socket that Paul could fit his stump into. Every time Paul needed one or two new sockets, which happened frequently as his muscles rebuilt and the legs changed in size, the procedure began again.

Finally, Mike screwed each socket to an artificial knee joint, and then attached that to a titanium pipe with an artificial foot wearing a lightweight hiking boot. When Paul pushed his stump into the socket, negative pressure kept the leg on by suction. For added security, each prosthesis had a thick cotton belt at the top that wrapped around Paul's pelvis. Mike brought the legs to show Paul as they were being assembled and tested. Paul liked the look of them. Made from carbon fibre, the legs looked strong.

In theory Paul was in recovery, but his schedule was frenetic. Aside from exhausting physio sessions twice a day, he faced other medical appointments and consultations, including counselling, with Glenrose health care workers. Officials with Veterans' Affairs and National Defence came by with medical and insurance forms.

A steady stream of visitors, both buddies from the base and friends from civilian life, kept arriving.

Simon came up to his room numerous times a week, a highlight for Paul, but these visits usually occurred at the end of the day when he was completely worn out. Father and son did quiet things together, such as homework, or drawing army guys or *Star Wars* characters. Paul had made a point of getting Simon hooked on *Star Wars* paraphernalia —video games, action figures, and movies. Paul loved the series of space adventure movies, and wanted to share the magic and mythology of Luke and the Jedi warriors with his son.

In the evenings, after Audra took Simon home for his bath and bed, Paul sat in his wheelchair at the desk in his room at the Glenrose. He had ordered a few military models on the Internet, detailed replicas of the military environment in Afghanistan. He enjoyed putting them together in peace and quiet. One model was a G-Wagon parked beside a mud and brick building, the kind of building you see throughout Kandahar. The model reminded Paul of the explosion, which already seemed like so long ago.

Other nights, Paul looked at photographs on his laptop in his room. He was putting together a slide show of his experiences in Afghanistan. He reviewed pictures of his medical kit, and a couple of photos of the G-Wagon, blackened and busted. Paul gazed at a snapshot of himself, before the explosion, lying on his side in his camouflage gear on the dusty ground, propped up on his elbow. In the photograph, a G-Wagon was parked in the background.

"I like the guy that I was before. He was a neat guy," Paul said. "I wouldn't mind being him again. But I'm a different person now, without a doubt. I know that person is a good person, but is he a good fit with Audra? Audra fell in love with me before. Will she fall in love with this new person? I don't know."

Since the accident, Paul had focused in a single-minded way on learning to walk again. The people around him—from the psychologist he saw at the Glenrose to his friends and family members—carefully asked him why it was important to be exactly like the man he was. Why did his legs matter when his soul was intact? Paul knew they had a point. At a deeper level, he recognized that he would never be the man he was before the explosion; that man disappeared on the streets of Kandahar on January 15, 2006, and no amount of strenuous effort would bring him back. Paul's determination to walk defied reason at times.

As the weeks of hospital treatment flowed one into the other, Paul's perspective shifted. By the time he left the University of Alberta hospital, he had shed his fear of dying. Here at the Glenrose, Paul faced a new challenge. How was he going to live? Like many people who had lost limbs before him, Paul had to deal with a simple, but profound question. Who was he now that his legs were gone? Paul wasn't at all sure of his identity without them. At his worst times, he suspected he wasn't much of anything if he couldn't stand tall.

As much as he paid lip service to creating a "new normal," it was clear from Paul's behaviour that the "new normal" needed to be quite a bit like the old normal, or he just wasn't having it.

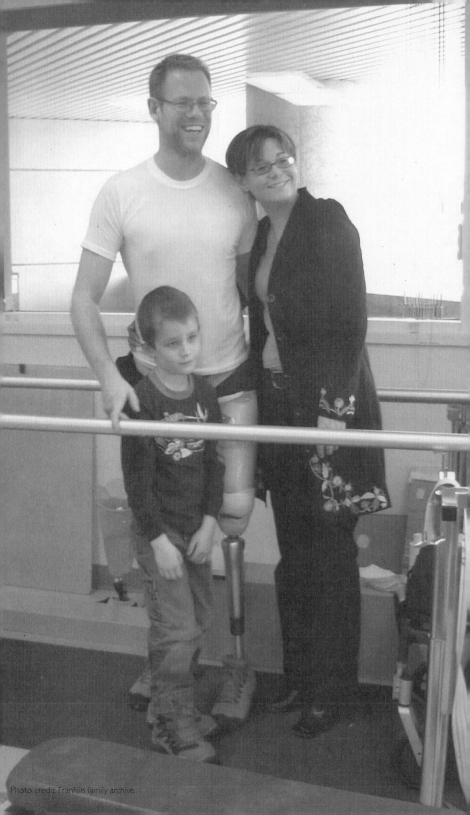

8

AUDRA'S WORLD

AUDRA WAS DOING SOME HEAVY LIFTING on the home front as Paul prepared himself, physically and emotionally, to begin a new life. The tiny house their family had purchased in downtown Edmonton in the fall of 2004 was not wheelchair accessible and it was not practical to renovate. Just after Paul moved to the Glenrose hospital, Audra bought a new house that was more than double the size, and twice the price, of the old one. The military had awarded Paul a $250,000 settlement for the loss of both legs. With that money, the Franklins put a big down payment on their new home and purchased a new car for Paul, a sporty navy-blue Mini Cooper with hand controls. Paul still banked his full salary as a master corporal, roughly $4,200 a month. He also received $3,200 a month for his injuries from Veterans Affairs, a lifetime pension that would be passed on to Audra if he was to die first. Officially, Audra was still working as an administrator at Oxford Properties Group, a commercial leasing firm. Since Paul's injury, however, the company had been more than generous, offering paid time off that allowed Audra to work when she could, but still be at Paul's side when she needed to be. Even though Paul and Audra were able to comfortably cross "money" off their list of worries, all the money in the world wasn't going to make things right.

Paul and Audra decided to purchase their new place in one of Edmonton's new housing developments located midway between their old house in a downtown neighbourhood and the Edmonton Garrison, just outside the northern city limits. The new development was in an area known as Griesbach, named after First World War hero Maj. Gen. William Griesbach of the 49th Battalion of the Canadian Expeditionary Force, later to become the Royal Edmonton Regiment. Maj. Gen. Griesbach, who died in 1945, was also a Mayor of Edmonton and a Member of Parliament. When the Franklins purchased their new show home in Griesbach, a charming two-storey with a fireplace and hardwood floors, they were pleased that it was just down the street from a big statue of Janet Griesbach, wife of the military commander, and an army nurse during the First World War.

Audra liked the neighbourhood's friendly atmosphere and its proximity to schools and shopping. Paul relished its military heritage. The Griesbach neighbourhood had been the home of the military base in Edmonton for some sixty years. In the mid-1990s, however, the Department of National Defence decided to combine the troops at Griesbach with Calgary forces in a new super-base set up at CFB Namao, located on the northern outskirts of Edmonton. Over the next few years, the Griesbach facilities and military families moved out to Namao, and the federal government turned the land at Griesbach over to a crown corporation. Working in conjunction with a private developer, the agency committed the land to housing, with a proviso that the site respects its military past. The development proved popular, with non-military families snapping up homes, eager to be part of the historic area.

Edmontonians had always rubbed shoulders with military families. Two generations of army families had lived and worked under the leafy spread of elms that arched across the streets of Griesbach. Because the base was not separate from the rest of the city, military and civilian families had much in common. Their kids played soccer and hockey together; everybody shopped at Sears. Soldiers remarked to each other that in other Canadian cities, they would think twice before wearing their uniforms off the base. Soldiers in Edmonton wore their work gear into Tim Horton's without worrying that someone would look down on them for it.

When local troops were deployed to Afghanistan, the city rallied around its soldiers and their families. In August of 2002, Edmonton hosted a parade to welcome home the first rotation of soldiers that had served overseas. Starting along the road from the Edmonton International airport, located on the southern ridge of the city, small crowds of people lined the streets into the capital city and up to the Canadian Forces base at Namao. As buses full of returning soldiers made their way north to the base, Edmontonians cheered and waved yellow ribbons along the route. Soldiers said the local support overwhelmed them.

When Paul was injured, Audra remembered how the community had backed its soldiers. That was part of the reason she and Paul decided to be so open with their story. They wanted to share their experience as a military family with the community that had been so generous to them.

Selling the old house and moving was a frantic process that started within days of the family's arrival back from Landstuhl at the end of January. Everyone helped. Faye remembered the crazy Friday in early February, shortly after the old house was listed, when the real estate agent called at 5:30 PM to say he was bringing over a potential buyer in ninety minutes. Audra was out, but Faye and a few friends were at the house, packing dishes and sorting through Simon's toys, separating the broken bits of action figures from the stuff that was still good. Suddenly, they were all in high gear.

"Andrew got dinner going. Amy went to clean the bathroom. I started sweeping and washing the kitchen floor, while Chad (Amy's husband) took out the garbage and swept and washed the back hall and basement steps," Faye recalled. Like a scene from a television home makeover show, the house was sparkling and the cleaners edging out the back way as the real estate agent entered the front door.

Although Audra had no shortage of help, her new life still felt like bloody hard work. She told herself that so long as Paul was in the hospital, she would treat the whole experience as if he was still away on tour. She was used to making Simon's lunches in the mornings, getting him off to school, and then heading to work. Her mother was a huge help, often bringing Simon home to her place for weekend sleepovers, picking him up after school, or taking him to tae kwon do.

Audra and Faye with the Franklin family dog, Hanna Grace.
Photo credit: Ian Scott

Now, on top of everything else, Audra had to get herself and Simon up to the hospital, usually daily, and also buy a new house while packing, cleaning, and selling the old one.

"It stinks," Audra said at the time. "I don't want to go to the hospital every day because it's tiring, but Simon and Paul need each other and I have to forget I'm tired and that I'd rather watch TV. I have to put that aside and be there for my boys."

Simon seemed to know when things had become too much for his mother. He told his grandma that it was okay if he didn't see Paul every day "because I have Daddy in my heart."

Audra also had to contend with a myriad of bureaucratic details involving the military and ongoing calls from the media. She was so dog-tired by the end of the day that she couldn't sleep. She conceded that while patience was a virtue, it had never been one of hers. Now she had even less of the quality than before.

"Overwhelmed and exhausted is the new normal," she said routinely when asked how she was doing.

For the first month after they came back from Germany, Audra rode on raw adrenaline. Paul's health was still precarious and he was struggling with the question about whether to keep the right leg. Audra was relieved when he reached a decision. She could quit living in limbo and move headlong into plans for the new house, including organizing a chair lift that could take Paul to the second floor. By March, however, the ups and downs of a new life had gutted Audra. She started to drag and would occasionally have what she describes as a "a major meltdown." She began to attend weekly mental health appointments with a therapist at Edmonton Garrison, which helped. Audra was dealing with a lot of anger. The war had turned her husband into a new person, someone she didn't even know sometimes. Audra missed the old Paul.

"I'm angry that I'm in this position. I'm angry that I have a disabled husband. But at the same time, I think I'm just mad at the situation, but not necessarily how the situation happened . . . I believe in what Paul was doing there, and I supported him in going. And I know he was just doing his job."

She coped the best way she could, accepting that a big old sob was sometimes the best option. Audra did find comfort in time with Paul and Simon. "And I tried to be positive a lot. Paul was very good at that, too. He has a great outlook. And you've got to trust and accept what's happening, so there was a lot of faith involved."

That faith wasn't necessarily in God, but in each other. Paul had to trust that Audra would do the right things when it came to Simon and the house. Audra had to know that Paul would make the right decisions about his leg, and that he would do the hard work necessary to get home again. As hard as everything was, Audra was proud of her husband.

"Paul has to work so hard for what he has. He's not a student; he breaks his neck for every single thing he does. So he's put his heart and soul into this career. And I'm proud of how he handled himself and how he shows Simon challenges . . . I always thought Paul was a great role model for Simon to have, but even more so now."

>>>

SPRING IN EDMONTON COMES IN FITS and starts. As the days become longer and brighter, winter relaxes and loosens its hold, only to grab hard again, sometimes within hours. Audra and Paul's moving day—Wednesday, March 15—was a classic spring day in the prairie city, dawning at minus fourteen degrees Celsius, but with a bright sun and blue sky that softened the snow by 3:00 PM, when the moving truck finally arrived at the new home. Of course, one of the three cats, Sammy, got out of the old house and could not be found. Faye and Simon wandered the old neighbourhood, calling his name. Audra could hardly be bothered to care; her energy for nurturing was at an all-time low and even feeding Chloe, Sammy,

Paul and Audra drink a toast in their new home on moving day in March 2006.

Photo credit: Franklin family archive

and Sydney sometimes felt like more than she could manage. All things considered, the day went well; Audra's boss at Oxford Properties Group kindly offered to pay for the move, which saved the Franklins a few thousand dollars. Paul came over from the Glenrose to tell the movers where to put things, and two of Audra's friends from work arrived around 4:00 PM to unwrap the breakables and organize the cupboards. Faye made sure that before she left that evening, the beds were made up with fresh sheets so Audra and Simon could enjoy a good night's rest in their new home.

Audra was happy and upbeat on moving day, and Faye was thrilled to see her daughter like that. She had been showing some signs of post-traumatic stress disorder, which is not uncommon among family members of those who have suffered a great loss. Audra endured blinding migraines and panic attacks. She dreamed about the explosion, even though she had not witnessed it. She saw Paul flying through the air in repetitive nightmares. On moving day, however, Audra's deep brown eyes sparkled just like the old days and her face softened. Faye bought a special guest book for the new house. After the pizza arrived, she passed the book around so the helpers could pen their best wishes for a new start for Paul and Audra.

The next day, Faye cleaned up at the old place before the new owners took possession. As she hauled a load of garbage out the back door, Sammy waltzed in, swinging his tail high in the air and sniffing about for something to eat. Faye alternately cursed and kissed the cat and then delivered him to his new home. Simon told Sammy that the kitty litter was now in the basement.

>>>

PAUL WASTED NO TIME IN GETTING home that weekend on his first pass from the Glenrose. He had mastered bumming up and down steps. He was tired of waking up at the rehab hospital, weary of the food and the colour of the walls. He couldn't wait to get into his own bed.

The first weekend pass reminded Audra of Paul's many homecomings after a military mission, a course or tour. Once again, she and Simon had created their own routine, and even though they wanted Paul at home, it always took a while to settle in. The first weekend Paul was home from the Glenrose was like that, but worse. As it turned out, the ramp that a friend had built from just outside the garage in the backyard up to the back door was too steep. Paul was humiliated that he couldn't wheel himself up. Audra found it hard to balance between helping her husband and trying not to be overbearing.

"Oh, it was so stressful," she said later, chuckling at the memory.

"Because I hovered. I didn't want to leave him alone in the bathtub because what if he drowned? He has no knees to stop himself from sliding . . . it was so awful."

Soon Audra discovered she didn't have to babysit her husband in the bathtub. She began to figure out what he needed help with, like getting out of the bathtub, and what he could do on his own— almost everything else.

Audra was always clear on one thing: she was never going to be her husband's nursemaid. "I've always said I would never be his caregiver. If he needed care given, we would hire someone to do that. That's not my job. My job is to be his wife, to be his friend, to hang out. He needs his privacy and his dignity."

Paul understood and agreed with Audra's perspective. Fiercely independent, he didn't want Audra's help with his personal needs. He was already worried about getting in the way at home. He cringed as his wheelchair banged against the fresh white baseboards in the living room and kitchen, scraping off the paint.

That first weekend at home was hard on everyone. Bumming up and down the long flight of stairs wore Paul out, and his beloved bed wasn't as comfortable as he remembered. After many months sleeping solo, both Paul and Audra had trouble being in the same bed again. The legs are a large skin surface from which the body can release heat, and since losing his lower extremities, Paul's body had a hard time cooling itself. Sleeping with Paul was like sleeping with a blast furnace, and by Sunday, Audra couldn't wait for her husband to go back to the hospital. She planned to go back to work full-time the next week, and needed to get organized. Simon, however, cried inconsolably when they dropped his dad off at the Glenrose after Sunday supper. All in all, it was a less than idyllic homecoming.

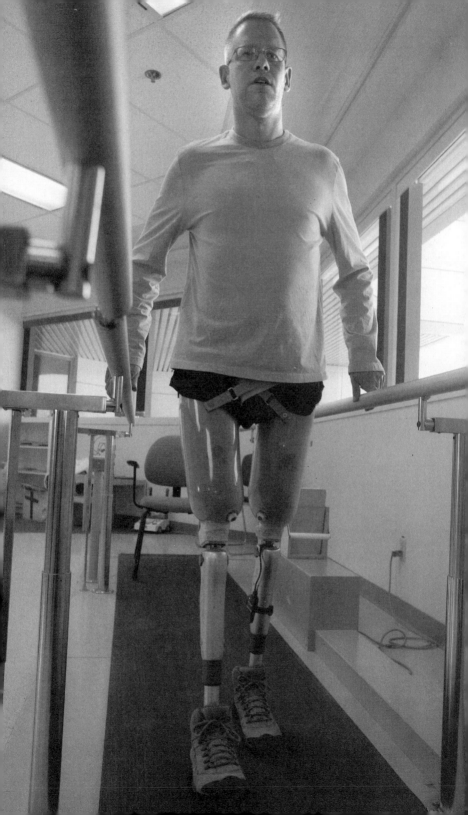

9

MY BODY, MY BATTLEFIELD

>>> MARCH 24, 2006

ON A FRIDAY AFTERNOON IN EARLY spring, Paul took his first step on prosthetic legs in the physiotherapy gym at the Glenrose. Audra stood by with the video camera, her stomach in knots.

Beforehand, Mike had helped Paul slide the sockets of the prostheses onto his stumps. A tight fit was important to keep the legs in place, to give Paul better control, and to distribute weight as evenly as possible to keep pressure off the tender tips of the stumps.

Learning to bend a prosthetic knee is an intricate procedure. For launch day, Mike and Bev suggested Paul keep the knees in a locked position, which was somewhat akin to walking on stilts. Paul was okay with that. He let Mike and Bev help him up out of his wheelchair, a tough transition when the knees don't bend. Then Paul stood still between the parallel bars and tried to balance. Bev was just behind him, holding onto a strap wrapped around Paul's waist so she could grab him if he fell forward. Paul gripped the side rails. His knuckles were white in contrast to the red burn scars on the backs of his hands.

He wavered at first. Looking straight ahead, Paul began to think about his muscles. He rocked sideways to get himself started, and heaved his trunk forward. Tightening his buttocks and concentrating hard on his thigh muscles, Paul swung one leg forward, then rested briefly before swinging the other leg to meet the first one. He walked like a penguin, from one end of the parallel bars to the other and back again, but he made it. His chest heaved from the aerobic effort.

Paul liked being upright. "Now I can look at people, in the eye, and get a sense of what I was," he said.

Right away he was ready to try again, this time with the knees unlocked. Bev and Mike agreed. The two always took Paul's lead in therapy, knowing his strong arms could support his entire weight if needed. With the knees unlocked, Paul managed to shift his weight so that the knee would come forward and bend, just a little. Then, haltingly, slowly, he struggled to the end of the bars and back. Twice. Sweat trickled from Paul's scalp, through his sideburns and down his cheeks. His shirt was wet with the effort. Audra looked astounded.

"It was weird because it was the first time he'd been upright," she said later. "I was so amazed at his tenacity. He was just exhausted, but really pleased with himself."

Paul collapsed into his wheelchair at the end of the physiotherapy session.

That's it, he said. I'm going home for the weekend.

Paul spent most of Saturday and Sunday in bed, sleeping while his body regained its strength. He told Audra that his stint between the parallel bars was harder than running twenty kilometres. Lying in his bedroom upstairs, listening to the murmur of his wife and son as they talked in the kitchen below, Paul had to admit something to himself: this walking business would be tougher than he expected.

Exhausted and in pain, he thought about what to do next. Instinctively, he knew. All of Paul's military training told him that if his task were to walk again, well, he'd better get up and get back at it. He thought about the war heroes he had read about, men who received the Victoria Cross for acts of bravery. While he did not place himself in that prestigious company, he remembered what war heroes inevitably said when journalists or historians or their own mothers asked them how they did it.

"They would say, 'I didn't do anything special. I just did what I had to do.' That's exactly the same with me. I just have to get better. There is no other reason."

Being a soldier put Paul in this purgatory. Being a soldier would get him out.

>>>

PEOPLE ASSUME THAT TECHNOLOGY CAN RESOLVE almost any challenge that human beings can invent. So you lose your legs, you'll get new ones, right? Aren't they doing amazing things with prosthetic technology these days? The average person can fail to appreciate that walking is a marvel that involves more than just the mind and body. In some ways, walking remains a mystery, even to doctors and scientists.

When we walk, we use our feet, our ankles, our knees, and our hips. Even standing still, we are always moving slightly, our ankles shifting and muscles twitching and firing to accommodate any number of challenges. The thickness of the carpet. A sore spot where a blister is rubbing. A fierce wind. If we reach for something, our leg muscles tighten and our knees lock so we don't fall over as our body follows the arm. Just standing on two full-length artificial legs is a feat of strength and endurance. The hips and trunk must do all the work of stabilizing the body on top of the prostheses. Moving is something else altogether. Think of a new driver sitting behind the wheel of the car. Everything looks easy until he or she slips the vehicle into gear.

No prosthetic unit has yet been able to replicate the interactions of the many small joints, muscles, and ligaments of the foot. The human foot gives back more than 250 per cent of the energy that the body puts into the step, serving up an enormous propulsive force to keep the process going. Even the most advanced prosthetic foot available, known as an energy-return foot, gives back less than 90 per cent of the energy that's put into it. A real foot creates energy; an artificial foot sucks it away.

The knee is also extremely complex, with a moving axis of rotation and not just a simple hinge. Prosthetic designers have yet to figure out how to replace the functions of shock absorption and rotation that occur in a natural leg. The adjustments that instantly occur in any joint or muscle are related to the ability of the body and the brain not just to control motion, but to sense what is happening in the limb. The feeling of where your leg is, whether your foot is flat on the floor, or you've just stepped on a pebble, are sensations unique to the human body. A stump can only get a vague sense of the outer world through contact with the socket of the prosthesis. Even the most advanced artificial legs are, as Mike often said, nothing more than a Yugo compared to the Jaguar.

Paul had another standard joke he delivered to visitors at the Glenrose. He said that his old legs were nearly shot anyway. His knees were damaged from too many long runs, and a number of toenails had virtually disintegrated due to his strenuous athletic pursuits. It was time to trade the old legs in for a new pair, went the joke. Of course, prostheses cannot begin to take the place of real legs, which move in sync with the hips, back, shoulders, and head in a subtle dance that creates the easy look and feel of the human gait.

Few of us perceive our bodies as a miracle of motion. Even as Paul joked about the run-down condition of his old legs, he was thinking hard about what they used to do for him. Carry him through a marathon. Steady his tall frame as he lifted Simon high up and over his shoulder.

Paul learns that while his new limbs are technically advanced, they can't replicate the miracle of the real thing.

Photo credit: Bruce Edwards

Recognizing the distance to recovery didn't stop Paul from being absolutely certain he would make it. When he needed inspiration, he looked at a snapshot taken in Banff a couple of years before the explosion, while he had been scrambling in the Rockies.

Sitting on a rocky outcropping near the summit of his hike, Paul had snapped a photograph of his legs from above, dangling in space. There were his knees, legs, and hiking boots, laced up tight, and a craggy field of boulders far below. He showed the photo to people who came by his room, and he told them about a guy named Warren Macdonald. Paul had heard that Macdonald had lost two legs above the knee in a climbing accident in Australia, but had fought back and was now able to do a modified form of mountain climbing. That's what Paul wanted to do, too. He also talked to Mike about ordering a bouncy, curved prosthetic foot that some amputee athletes used for running.

Paul took a photograph of his own legs and feet after scrambling up Mount Cascade in Banff National Park in the spring of 2005.

Photo credit: Franklin family archive

"Right from the beginning, he was going to not just walk, but run," recalled Bev. "I thought, I don't want to burst your bubble, but you have no idea how hard this is."

At the beginning of April, the C-Legs arrived. Each lithium-ion powered leg can run for thirty hours before needing a recharge. A computer chip reads the walker's pace and allows the leg to swing, using hydraulics. The chip calculates the walking speed, the amount of weight pushing on the toe, and the pitch of the walking surface some fifty times a second. This constant monitoring helps the C-Leg adjust to make stairs, curbs, or slopes easier to negotiate.

The remarkable thing about C-Legs is the knee. Walkers have to learn how to "load the toe," that is, to put 70 per cent of maximum pressure on the toe, which will trigger the knee to bend. Applying that pressure while keeping the other leg stable is a difficult trick, especially when the second leg is also prosthetic. It took Paul a month of physio, twice a day, to be able to smoothly step, foot to foot.

Still, Paul made rapid progress once fitted with the new leg units. With the old legs, Paul walked ten metres outside the parallel bars, wearing forearm crutches, in fifty-eight seconds. Within a couple of weeks of getting the C-Legs, Paul had cut his time by nearly half, walking the same distance in thirty-three seconds. Bev placed objects in his way, such as a piece of foam or a length of carpet, so Paul could walk on different surfaces. Then she upped the ante with a cane and a block of wood. Paul learned to throw his leg up and over the obstacles. On April 28, Paul walked two hundred metres, once around the second floor hallways, with arm crutches. He still had Bev at his back with the strap; the physiotherapist's arms were tight and sore every single day with the effort of steadying her patient.

Getting up from a sitting position was gruelling for Paul. He and Bev worked for hours at the skill. Paul sat on the edge of the bed in the gym, manipulating his crutches or a walker to help him

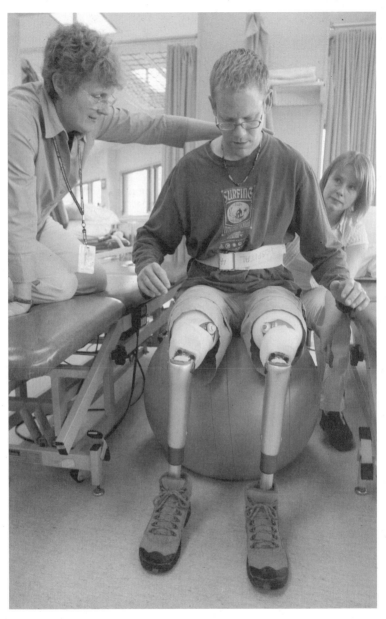

Bev offers support to Paul as he tries to balance while wearing his new legs. At right is physiotherapy student Mandy Rempfer.

Photo credit: Bruce Edwards

lever up with one straight leg. Sitting down was also an art. With real legs, the knees lower gently, but Paul found himself frequently crashing as he moved from standing to sitting with the C-Legs. It was strenuous and often disheartening work.

"The fight that I am in now is sometimes harder than all those things I did in the past. Climbing mountains, running marathons, even being in Afghanistan. Sometimes getting out of a car is just as hard. In some ways, almost as dangerous," Paul said during this stressful time. "I was once asked if I had a fear of falling. In reality, it's not a fear of falling, but a fear of hitting my head and paralyzing myself. The last thing I need is another trip to the hospital. Another rehab time. Another surgery."

Frequently, visitors came to watch Paul practice walking. Friends, the padre from the base, army officials, or family members would wander into the gym to observe his progress. Paul saw it as his duty to make himself available to all comers. Having placed himself and his family in the eye of the media, he felt an obligation to play the role of the chipper recovering soldier. Paul's motivation increased as the number of dead and wounded soldiers rose in the early months of 2006. Polls suggested Canadians were growing more concerned about the military's role in Afghanistan. A poll conducted by Strategic Counsel for CTV and the *Globe and Mail* in May suggested 54 per cent of the Canadian public opposed troop deployment, up 13 per cent from a similar poll conducted two months earlier.

More than ever, Paul wanted Canadians to know what soldiers were made of. He also wanted his country to support the mission as the pressure grew on his comrades in Afghanistan. Paul never said no to a press interview, or admitted to anything more than a passing problem, one that was sure to disappear soon. "How's it going?" visitors asked, and it was always going just fine. That was the only answer Paul would allow himself.

He tried to minimize the emotional strain of his therapy by refusing to think too hard about it. When he felt sad, he just pushed himself past it. Putting one foot ahead of the other was more than a metaphor for Paul. Though he found anniversary dates—one month, two months, three months from the explosion—particularly hard, he knew sad or angry feelings were just going to take away the energy he needed to get the job done. People were always talking to him about the importance of grieving, of working through the denial and the anger. Paul felt he could do those things later if necessary.

"(When) your emotions get involved, then the physical body just doesn't work as well and that deteriorates the whole rehab," he said. "That's why the emotional part is so important in rehab. Because without your head on straight, you'll never be able to walk."

In a rare unguarded moment, Paul reveals the anguish of straining to walk on his artificial legs.

Photo credit: Bruce Edwards

Bev could see that it was tough for Paul to keep swallowing the emotional and physical aching. He never broke down during physical tasks, no matter how painful and gruelling they became. Occasionally, there would be a day when he was waiting for a phone call that didn't come. Then food service was late with his lunch tray, or he didn't get his pain medication on time. Bev saw the cracks.

"Not many guys can cry with a woman," she said. "But afterwards he would apologize and I would say forget it and he would be able to move on."

Bev felt good about providing a safe place for Paul to heal. She knew it was tough being a hero all the time. "And once you set yourself up for that, it's hard to know how to deal with a day when you're just feeling down about things."

Paul knew Canadians described him as a hero, even though he had never saved anyone. He wondered if it was because they shared a yearning for someone to rise above the ordinary, to take the lead.

"I think in this day and age, we don't have as many heroes as we'd like, so people lose sight of what true heroism is and so they put what I've done down as heroic," he said in a reflective moment.

Paul did acknowledge there was something profound about his own experience, something worth sharing.

"I didn't fight off ten Taliban or charge a trench with a bayonet. My heroism has, in a sense, been here in Canada as I try to recover."

He believed anybody could be a hero. He thought of the soldier, Jake Petton, who ran to Paul's side and applied the life-saving tourniquet. That made Jake a hero in Paul's eyes, even if the young soldier's efforts were largely overlooked. Paul believed there was room for the heroic in day-to-day life.

"It's tenacity and strength of character that saves your butt," he said. He lived that credo every day.

Paul meets with friends and colleagues at Edmonton Garrison in the spring of 2006.

>>>

BY THE END OF APRIL, PAUL knew he was ready to start wearing his legs in public. He found his first chance at a memorial service for Pte. Robert Costall, a twenty-two-year-old gunner with the 1st Battalion, PPCLI, who had been killed at the end of March in Afghanistan. Paul arrived at the service in his wheelchair, but with his legs on. Though Audra had to help him out of the chair, Paul stood with his arm crutches for part of the ceremony. Joining his colleagues in a tribute, and answering reporters' questions while wearing his new legs, boosted Paul's confidence, and he wanted more. Another opportunity came soon enough. Canada's Governor General, Michaelle Jean, was flying to Edmonton at the beginning of May. She was commander-in-chief of the Canadian Forces, and asked for a private meeting with Paul and the other wounded Edmonton soldiers. Paul wondered if the suit he wore to his wedding would still fit. He had lost fifty pounds since he last tried it on.

Photo credit: Bruce Edwards

1O

ABOUT SIMON

IF THERE WAS A SMALL SAG in the Franklin family's mask of determination, it was Simon. Paul and Audra had done everything they could to make life easier for Simon, and yet he was now a different boy. Audra, an avid reader, had pored over books such as *Children and Trauma: A Guide for Parents and Professionals,* looking for clues. Faye thought maintaining a consistent routine and sticking to the rules would help, but she too struggled with Simon's behaviour. Always an easygoing child, Simon now "pitched a fit," in his grandmother's words, when things did not go his way. Sometimes he refused to eat. His attention span at school was short and his marks suffered. Faye wondered if Simon should see a therapist. Maybe he needed to cry more often, or cry harder.

Oh, he's cried, Audra assured her mother.

I think he spends too much time in front of those video games, Faye said. Her daughter was silent. There was a lot happening in their lives. It was hard to know what was going on in Simon's head. He was just a small boy adjusting to a big change.

Born on June 24, 1999, Simon Marshall Franklin came into the world weighing six pounds, thirteen ounces. He was 21.5 inches long. Bottle-fed, Simon slept well as an infant and didn't cry much.

"Oh, he had his opinions," his mother laughed as she described his babyhood. "But he was a good boy."

When Simon was six weeks old, his father went away to Camp Borden for medical training and didn't come home again, except for a brief Christmas vacation, until his son was ten months old. Audra told Simon that he was luckier than many other boys whose fathers were soldiers, because his dad was there when Simon was born.

From the time he was big enough to sit up and reach for toys, Simon loved his big fire truck and his ambulance, as well as a set of wooden blocks. His father read *The Hobbit* to him when he was still a baby. Simon seemed to appreciate the tale, watching his dad closely through eyes that were a shade of blue-green, like the sea. His favourite stories as a preschooler were the adventures of *Thomas the Tank Engine*.

Simon developed a fondness for foods that were blue when he was a toddler. His mom called it "Simon's Blue Period." He liked blueberry yogurt, blue Fruit Roll-Ups, and blue oatmeal, which his mother made with a special potion called food colouring. He would eat these things from a blue plastic bowl with blue utensils.

Once, when Simon was about three, he needed new rubber boots. His parents took him to the store and told him to pick between a red pair and a blue pair. Simon put one boot on each foot and then looked in the mirror for a long time.

"My choose, my like, my want," he said over and over as he studied the boots from different angles.

Simon had his first GI Joe by the age of three and after that, he played a lot with army toys. Simon's toy box overflowed with helicopters, helmets, and guns. Tanks of different sizes and colours lined the shelf on his bed.

Simon studied at a German immersion preschool when he was four, because his mother had gone to high school briefly in Germany and learned to speak the language. Simon was not so keen on learning

German. He went to kindergarten at St. Angela's in Edmonton when he was five, because that's where his babysitter's children went. Then he got a new babysitter, so he switched schools. On the first day of Grade One, Simon walked with his mother over to Norwood School, a downtown school closer to his home. He had to change schools again when they bought the new house after Paul returned from Afghanistan.

Simon knew why his father went to Afghanistan; it was so that one day, little Afghan girls would be allowed to go to school like Simon and his friends and little Afghan boys would be able to fly their kites.

Simon was a good student at school, especially in math and science, but he liked recess best because he liked to play with his friends. His best friends in Grade One were Stevie, Braden, Kyle, and a different Kyle.

Science programs on Discovery Channel intrigued Simon. He also liked to watch documentaries and war stories on History Channel with his dad. He still flipped the channel to the silly shows on TV, such as SpongeBob SquarePants cartoons. He was fascinated with pyramids and all things Egyptian.

Tacos were among Simon's favourite foods, along with grilled cheese sandwiches, without the crusts, and salad. He never had much of a sweet tooth—his parents had to encourage him to nibble away at his Halloween candy—but he loved oatmeal cookies and ginger cookies. He made banana bread when he had sleepovers at his grandma Faye's place.

Simon wouldn't go to sleep at night without Scorch, a scruffy beanbag dragon—that is, until Paul gave him a soft stuffed camel he'd found in Dubai, which wasn't too far from Afghanistan. Brown Eyes arrived in time for Christmas, when Simon was six. The summer after his father came back from Afghanistan, the little camel was accidentally left behind in a hotel in Glacier National Park.

Paul and Audra called the hotel, and the hotel said they would mail the camel to Edmonton, but Brown Eyes was never seen again. Paul told Simon that Brown Eyes was on his own journey.

When Paul was hurt, Simon asked to see his father's leg, which was puffy and black and red, even before his mother would look at it.

Simon didn't feel much like eating in the months after his dad came home. He poked at his tacos at dinner, or shoved his grilled cheese sandwich around his plate. School started to irritate Simon; sometimes the other kids talked in class and it was hard to get his work done. At recess, it was windy. He started getting headaches from the noise and the wind.

After his dad lost his legs, Simon stopped talking about wanting to be a medic when he grew up. He still wanted to be in the army, though. He still wanted to go on missions.

The family got a new suv after his dad was hurt. It was called a Hyundai Sante Fe, with hand controls so his dad could drive with no legs. Simon remembered the day they picked up the new vehicle. There was a party at the dealership and Simon was supposed to be at school, but he had a headache. Simon told his teacher, and then his grandma came and got him and took him to the party. There were a lot of television cameras, and his parents were talking to reporters and people wearing suits. Simon's dad wore shorts and everybody looked at his new legs. Simon ran to his dad when he arrived and hugged him around the legs. Then he had some pop. Simon crawled around in the new vehicle, which smelled clean.

"Why was your head hurting, Simon?" his dad asked.

"All the kids were yelling in my ear," Simon said.

There were a lot of special parties after his dad was hurt. There was even a party at breakfast, which was too early as far as Simon was concerned. That's where he met the Governor General, Michaelle Jean, who was pretty and wore a leather skirt and jacket.

The Franklin family meets with Governor General Michaëlle Jean in May 2006 at the Officer's Mess, Canadian Forces Base Edmonton.

Photo courtesy of MCpl. Issa Paré, Rideau Hall

His mom said the suit was violet, but Simon thought it was purple. The morning of the breakfast party, his dad got mad at Simon because he was watching cartoons while he ate his cereal. Simon didn't understand because he always ate his cereal in the morning while watching cartoons. His mom got mad at his dad, and Simon felt badly. When Simon met the Governor General, he said hello in a polite voice like his parents told him. Then he snuggled into his mom and she picked him up. The Governor General rubbed Simon's back and his T-shirt went up and down. When it was over, Audra gave Simon a big hug and said she was proud of him.

Simon turned seven the summer after his dad was hurt. They had a birthday picnic in a leafy park in Edmonton's river valley with lots of kids and parents. His dad rode in his wheelchair because walking

Paul and Simon have a mock sword fight with pencils in the family kitchen.

Photo credit: Bruce Edwards

with his new "bionical" legs at the park would have been hard. There were lots of people and kids running, and his dad might fall down.

Before his dad was hurt, Simon spent a lot of time skateboarding with him. After he was hurt, they played with remote control cars, action figures, and video games. Simon liked to snuggle up with his dad in his leather chair and watch *Star Wars* movies or *Indiana Jones*. They did that before, too.

Simon knew a book was being written about his dad's mission in Afghanistan, and how he learned to walk again after losing his legs. He knew his parents and grandparents had all been interviewed for the book. Simon was asked what it had been like for him since his dad lost his legs in Afghanistan. He only thought for a moment before he quietly murmured.

"It's really usual. It's the same."

Photo credit: Bruce Edwards.

11

THE HOMECOMING

PAUL DID NOT EXPECT TO EXPERIENCE his rebirth in a dull grey cement parking lot, but that's where it happened. One week before his scheduled discharge date on May 17, Paul walked around the perimeter of the underground lot at the Glenrose hospital. It took him more than half an hour and wore him out for the rest of the day, but he managed to travel eight hundred metres on arm crutches without Bev trailing behind him like a mother nervously monitoring the slow progress of a determined tot. It was his longest walk ever. In the days that followed, Paul traded his arm crutches for two canes (this time with Bev at the ready). Wearing his legs up to six hours a day, he began to tackle grass and bumpy pavement. Then he learned to tilt, slowly, up a ramp.

"The goals we set on admission were that by the time he was discharged, Paul could walk one hundred metres with crutches, that he have a high level of wheelchair skills, and could get his own legs on and off," Bev recalled.

By discharge, Paul had met and exceeded those goals. He could get up from the floor, hanging onto a piece of furniture, with his legs on. He could get in and out of the car, with or without legs. He had mastered the hand controls in the family's new four-by-four vehicle.

It was a quiet triumph, barely noticed in the world around him, and only a few people understood its significance. In his book *Blood Brothers*, TIME senior correspondent Michael Weisskopf shared the story of losing his own hand in Iraq in December 2003, weaving his experience with the stories of three American soldiers who also lost limbs. Weisskopf said that one way to define heroism is as a quick response to a changing environment.

Paul read an excerpt of the book and it spoke to him in many ways. He knew about the need to respond quickly to change, and for him, too, it was a survival issue. Learning to walk was like needing to breathe. Without a sturdy pair of legs to carry him through his life, Paul felt he would suffocate, wither, and disappear.

On May 17, four months and two days after having his legs blown to bits in Kandahar, Paul checked out of the hospital on two prosthetic limbs. Although he would return to the Glenrose for physiotherapy for the next several months, it would be as an outpatient.

Paul could not wait to move on. "I want to go home. I really want to go home. It's tiring. I had a six-month tour and I had four months in the hospital. It's been a year. A year away from home and a normal life. I want to get back to it. Get back to doing things I like to do."

Paul rose early to pack his bags on the morning of his departure. He showed up as usual in the gym for his physio at 10:30 AM. At the last minute, there were problems. Bev said Paul's stride was way off and he was "waddling like a duck."

"You'll get a sore back over time. You're in the army. Don't they make you stand up straight?"

Paul rolled his eyes and called her a physioterrorist, but he knew she was right. Something felt stuck; Paul's toe was dragging when he took a step. The tip of one leg throbbed with pain. Paul sat down on a chair while Mike adjusted the leg.

"You've got an asymmetrical step," he said. "I think it's a valve issue."

Paul sighed. With artificial legs, there was always something. He remembered another day at physio. He had spent the previous evening out with friends, drinking beer and eating potato chips. The next morning, he couldn't get his thighs into the prosthetic sockets; the liquor and salt had led to swelling. Paul had to drink a lot of water and then wait for the tissue-expanding extras to be flushed from his system before he could get his legs back on.

Two weeks earlier, Paul had spent the morning in the Syncrude Centre for Motion and Balance, one of only two highly specialized labs in Canada able to take a microscopic look at the gait of people with prosthetic limbs. In the gait lab, Dr. Jackie Hebert helped attach a series of small black markers to Paul's C-Legs. The markers gave out signals picked up by sensors stationed around the lab. As Paul trudged through the room, red lights flashed like *Star Wars* laser sabres, picking up the minute machinations of his gait. With the information collected, experts in the lab looked at clues such as how much of Paul's weight was borne by his arms, with the help of crutches, and how much was supported by his legs, and how smoothly the legs were moving. The goal was to monitor and improve Paul's walking over time and to improve the function of the C-Legs so walking would be more comfortable, efficient, and manageable.

That day at the gait lab, Paul was tired and moved slowly. A sheen of sweat formed on his forehead. Jackie congratulated Paul on his efforts and his ongoing progress, but in a quiet way. As a specialist in rehabilitation medicine, she straddled the line between encouraging Paul's efforts and being honest about the limitations of the body. It was not exactly true that Paul could do anything he set his mind to. There was an end point.

"The more he uses his muscles, the stronger they get. But they can only do it for so long," she said. "The distance he will cover and his speed is limited by the maximum capacity of those muscles."

During that session in the gait lab, Paul shared a secret dream with Jackie.

"I'd love to try and be a soldier again. If I could do the military fitness test, I could prove I am the person I was."

Part of the military fitness test involved a thirteen-kilometre hike with a full pack.

"Is the test time limited?" Jackie asked.

"It has to be done in two hours and twenty minutes."

The doctor listened, nodded.

"It's always good to have goals," she said.

For Jackie, Paul was the patient of a lifetime. She had learned a lot from him about what willpower could achieve. She was careful not to focus on walking as the sole objective of rehabilitation. While other specialists had doubted Paul would be able to walk on prostheses—and told him so—from the first time Jackie met the soldier at the University of Alberta Hospital, she knew he would be successful. That's because he was young, strong, and absolutely focused on his goal.

"From that moment, I could see he was clearly very on top of things despite being on morphine in an acute surgical bed. I had a sense this person was going to push the envelope, and I was going to do absolutely everything I could do support that from a rehab point of view."

For Jackie, success wasn't just about walking. While Paul saw walking, running, and mountain climbing on prostheses as the goals, Jackie saw a bigger picture. She wanted Paul to use his C-Legs as one of several ways to make his life better. Over time, she hoped he would embrace a variety of ways of getting around, depending on the situation. Wheelchairs were best for airports and other busy places where the risk of being bumped is high. Stubbies—shorter

Paul stands beside a G-Wagon at Edmonton Garrison.

Photo credit: Bruce Edwards

legs with no knee joints—would make getting around the house easier by providing more stability so Paul could stand at the kitchen counter and cut vegetables. Arm crutches and C-Legs would work best if he were outside on an uneven sidewalk or grass. Canes, the least stable walking aid, were fine for inside and smooth surfaces.

"It's absolutely a success to be wearing the legs to access places and do things and stand when you want to stand, but you're not going to be walking around for an eight-hour workday. It would be too difficult and the muscles would fatigue and you'd be exhausted all the time. . . . So if Paul can see the value of using his wheelchair, of using his legs, of using the stubbies, then on any day, he can choose to use any of those things to accomplish his goals. That is the actual success: the fact that he can function completely independently in his home and in the community using whatever means are at his disposal."

In Jackie's mind, psychological adaptation and acceptance were the key. For some people, that evolution was a lifelong process.

"I think part of it is that a person needs to evolve from a psychological perspective to understand that who they are is inside, not the external appearance. And that's something that some people never get to."

>>>

BY NOON ON MAY 17, AUDRA arrived at the Glenrose from work, anxious to take her husband home. There was a mighty bustle as Audra and Faye helped Paul load the Sante Fe with his wheelchair, his computer, and his suitcases. Mike was touched when Paul gave him the model he had created of the G-Wagon on the streets of Kandahar as a parting gift. Mike knew he would miss Paul as a patient, and so would others in the physiotherapy gym.

"He was always encouraging to the other patients and he was

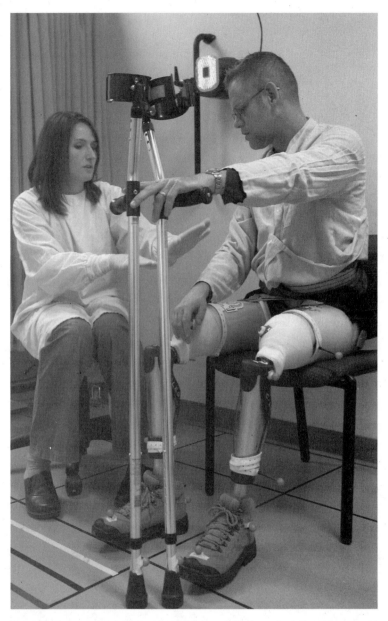

Rehabilitation specialist Dr. Jackie Hebert and Paul meet at the Glenrose to monitor Paul's progress.

Photo credit: Bruce Edwards

great to have around that way. They were always in awe of this guy, because he was so young and strong and he was in the paper and he was a nice guy. Everyone called him The Soldier, but he was so much more than a soldier. He was so amiable, and confident and willing to help. That's who Paul is. He's much more than a patient focusing on his own problems."

While at the Glenrose, Paul began working with Jackie to create a new charity, the Northern Alberta Amputee Program, or NAAP. Paul suggested the idea after he noticed Jackie struggling to find funding for things she wanted to do at the hospital. The goal of the new organization is to raise money for research into new prosthetic technology and surgical procedures for amputees, as well as new treatment and training methods, such as teaching amputees to run with a specialized running prosthesis. They also hope to provide access to education and support for amputees and their families.

The day Paul checked out, Audra was prepared to drive him home. Instead, Paul took the wheel, swinging out of the parking lot and onto the busy road in front of the hospital, driving with the hand controls. It was the first time he had driven in traffic since his explosion, and it made him nervous. Paul wanted badly to be safe again in his own living room.

At the house, Paul wheeled into the garage. A CBC television documentary crew waited there to record the homecoming. The camera focused on Paul as he swivelled his hips from the front seat of the car, then pulled his legs out. Audra headed back to the trunk, yanked out the wheelchair, and brought it to the driver's side of the car. Paul heaved himself into the chair and began to wheel toward the house. Faye had tied a big yellow ribbon to the light at the back porch, and she smiled when Paul noticed the symbol of welcome for a soldier returning from war. Inside, a bottle of champagne chilled in the fridge. But even as Paul entered the sanctuary of his own kitchen, he heard some bad news. The radio reported another

Paul pulls a bloody signal flag from inside the helmet he was wearing when injured in Afghanistan.

Photo credit: Bruce Edwards

Canadian soldier had been killed in Afghanistan. This time the soldier was a woman, the first Canadian female combat soldier to die in battle. Audra grabbed the telephone to see if she could find out the unidentified soldier's name, hoping it would not be one of their friends. Paul pulled out his Blackberry to check for messages. The war stayed with them.

>>>

THE NEXT MORNING, PAUL WOKE UP before 6:00 AM. It was show and tell at Simon's school, and Paul wanted plenty of time to get up, shower, and shave. He was nervous. He did not feel like breakfast, and was content to watch Simon as he slurped a bowl of cereal and milk in front of the cartoons on television. Audra took care of hustling Simon upstairs after breakfast to get dressed. Paul wheeled himself over to where his legs stood propped against the wall. Then he began the laborious process of working his stumps into the sockets, strapping the belts around his waist, and preparing to walk. He could hear Simon upstairs, Audra coaxing him to hurry, but Paul said nothing, determined not to disrupt their routine on this momentous day. He took a deep breath and looked at a three-tiered glass cabinet in the corner of the room, which Paul had put together as a kind of shrine to his time in Afghanistan. On the top shelf was a photo of Paul and a fellow soldier on a bright sunny day, the Afghan desert spread out behind them like a sandy blanket beneath a blue sky. In front of the photo stood the good luck charm that had graced Paul's G-Wagon—Jenna, the hula girl. Her grass skirt was singed, her ukulele burned. Paul's eyes moved downward, to the shelf that contained his two war medals. Below that, on the bottom shelf, was a model of a G-Wagon and Paul's helmet, with its medic brassard, a red cross. After Paul was injured, his buddy Jason had snagged the helmet. Jason promised his superiors he would return the helmet with the rest of Paul's military kit so it could be cleaned up before eventually making its way back to Canada. But Jason knew Paul wouldn't want that. So he hid the helmet in his own pack and when he returned to Canada at tour's end, he gave it back to Paul, just the way it was on the day of the suicide bombing. The helmet was still mud-streaked, its green canvas cover ripped.

Paul's reverie was disturbed when Simon clambered down the stairs. Audra was right behind him, stuffing her son's agenda book into his backpack. Simon was ready. Audra grabbed her purse and coat.

Good luck, she said, giving them both a hug.

With a flurry, Audra was out the door to work. Paul wheeled over to the fridge, grabbed a juice box, and put it in Simon's lunch. Simon slipped his backpack over his shoulders and got his dad's

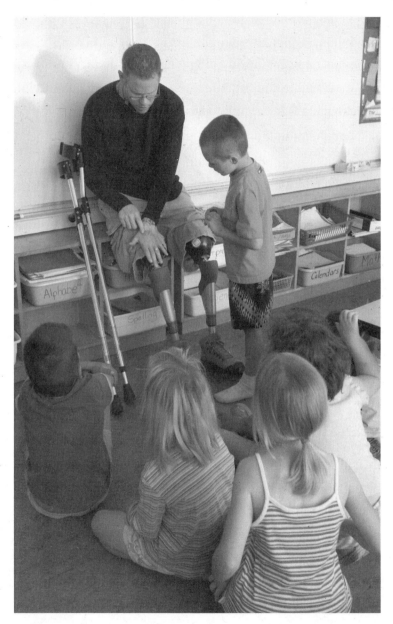

On the day that Simon brings his dad to class for show and tell, Paul explains to the schoolchildren how his artificial legs work.

Photo credit: Bruce Edwards

crutches. The two went out the back door, down the plywood ramp, and into the garage. Simon pushed the button for the garage door and the close, warm darkness of the garage soon welcomed the bright morning sun. It was shortly after 8:00 AM and Simon had to be at school, just a few blocks away, in forty minutes. Paul struggled up from the wheelchair and Simon handed him his crutches.

Okay Simon, Paul said. Let's go.

Photo credit: Rick MacWilliam

EPILOGUE

PREPARING FOR THE FIRST ANNIVERSARY OF the suicide attack, Paul decided he would take the day off from his desk job at 1 Field Ambulance, where he had been working part-time since the fall. He felt safer at home. He needed time to think. He needed solitude.

Paul changed his mind when the morning came. When he woke up, he knew he couldn't allow himself to stay inside. This was not a day for self-indulgence. He realized he had to go out into the world to prove, if only to himself, that he wasn't afraid. He got up, showered, and drove to work at the base. When he got there, he realized he had not shaved. Paul apologized to his superior officer for the stubble. His boss said: You made it. That's the important part.

Paul knew that getting to work was only the first challenge the day would present. Jeff and Will had asked Paul to meet them later at a sports bar called Jox, near the base. A bunch of military and civilian friends and family members planned to gather for a celebration. Jeff and Will wanted to toast their shared achievement: one year after their devastating injuries, the three were still alive, and together. Paul did not want to go to the pub party. He did not want to tell the story again, or review the details of a difficult year. He knew he had to go.

Audra, too, had planned to spend the anniversary of the bombing in the comfort of her home. It was a cold, grey day in the hardest part of an Edmonton winter, and she had the flu. Although she had managed to make it downstairs to sit on the couch in the living room, clutching a tissue, with her knees tucked up to the side, Audra was hardly in the mood to party. Hanna Grace, the family's new Basset Hound, snuffled around the edges of the red and camel-coloured carpet on the hardwood. Every so often, Audra reached down to rub the dog's silky coat.

Paul's father, Ron, was visiting from Calgary. A natural handyman, Ron had come to frame the basement for a guest room, bathroom, and family room. As Audra sat on the couch, Ron hammered two-by-fours into place in the basement. Wham. Wham. Wham. The whole house shook. Audra's hands flew to her ears as the scream of a power saw echoed through her home.

Sometimes Audra wondered if buying this home had been the best idea. Maybe a bungalow would have been better than a two-storey. A lift carried Paul to the second floor, but the basement was more or less off limits to him. Sure, he could "bum" down the stairs, but Paul hated getting around that way. It placed him too low to the ground and he did not like to be seen in that position. Bumming also meant that Paul couldn't use his hands for other things. Once, he bummed down to the basement to search for something in one of the many unpacked boxes, only to discover that the cats had urinated outside the litter box. He knew that in order to clean up the mess, he would have to make numerous trips back up the stairs to fetch cleaning supplies. How would he even carry them downstairs? He would have to find a backpack somewhere. There might be one on the top shelf of the hall closet, but he couldn't reach it. He felt so angry and helpless that he cried. When Faye arrived, he asked if she would mind cleaning up the cat pee.

Faye didn't mind, of course. Paul minded. As for Audra, she was looking at her dream home with new perspective.

>>>

THE PARKING LOT AT JOX SPORTS BAR was rutted and greasy with packed snow and ice. Paul decided not to wear his C-Legs, because he knew he could not negotiate that parking lot. He arrived at the front door in his wheelchair, only to discover unexpected barriers. Staff members could not find the restaurant's portable wheelchair ramp, and that stopped Paul from reaching the bar where his friends had gathered. The server was embarrassed and apologetic. She explained that construction workers were renovating Jox—giant sheets of plastic curtained off parts of the bar—and perhaps the workers had moved the wooden ramp. It's okay, Paul repeated several times. He sat with a small group of friends in a different part of the bar near the pool tables and electronic games, but there wasn't enough space for the large group. Eventually, a couple of Paul's brawny friends lifted him and his wheelchair into the raised section of the bar. Now the party could get started.

Jeff handed out cigars like a man with a new baby. One year earlier, the soldier had been lying in a sewer ditch on the streets of Kandahar, with a severe head injury that threatened to take his life. At one point, Jeff's brain swelled so dramatically that surgeons removed a piece of his skull to relieve the pressure. They sewed it inside his abdomen until the brain returned to its normal size and the piece of skull could be set back in place.

To look at Jeff—a tall, gregarious man with armloads of tattoos—you would not know doctors had once said he had stood a better than even chance of dying. His recovery, although remarkable, was far from complete. Jeff was back at work only two days a week at 1 Combat Engineer Regiment. The rest of the time, he attended an outpatient program at the Glenrose Hospital, for physiotherapy and classes in speech therapy, memory, and communications. Jeff's hearing is half what it used to be in one ear and he wears glasses, which he did not wear before the explosion. His long- and short-term memory is erratic. Jeff expects to receive a medical discharge from the military at some point. He is not deployable and according to military policy, all members of the Canadian Forces must be ready for battle.

Sitting in the pub, Jeff's fiancé, Julie Duncan, told friends about visiting Jeff at the University of Alberta Hospital when he was newly injured. The two had broken up before he went to Afghanistan, but Jeff had forgotten that. One day, after he started being able to speak again, Jeff looked at Julie and said that he couldn't remember her in his head but he remembered her in his heart.

Of the three soldiers, Will, now a corporal, was perhaps the least affected by the bomb blast. Although he had fractures in his right arm, a spinal cord injury, and a head injury, Will was back at PPCLI headquarters working part-time within a month of checking out of the hospital at the end of February 2006. He was working full-time by May. Will does not consider himself fully fit; his short and long-term memory are permanently damaged, and he speaks more slowly than he used to. His head injury could cause problems that might not show up for years. For now, his health was stable. Will had signed another three-year contract with the military.

"Why wouldn't I?" He hopes to return to Afghanistan before the mission ends.

"I've talked to lots of guys who have been injured and there are multiple reasons we want to go back," he says. "For one, we never got to finish the job, and that's a big thing in the military, to finish what you started. Also, you feel bad that you somehow failed your comrades. You to want another chance to prove yourself and to show you aren't afraid."

At the bar, Julie passed around a photo album of clippings she had collected about the explosion. She put it together for Jeff and decorated it with glittery hearts and sentimental stickers.

Other friends told Jeff, one more time, what happened the day of the suicide bombing. You gave your blast blanket away to wrap around that unexploded ordinance, remember? Jeff shook his head. Nope. Usually, soldiers sit on a protective blanket while on patrol in their vehicles, which helps shield them in case of an explosion. That day, Jeff had given his blast blanket to an Afghan police officer to wrap around some bombs the officer needed to transport. Paul had shoved his own blast blanket away from his feet that day because the blanket got in the way of driving. He used to think about that but he doesn't anymore.

Dressed in a black warm-up jacket and jeans with the cloth legs tucked under, Paul showed X-rays of his thigh bones, captured on his Blackberry, to anyone who was interested. His father, Ron, took a good look, as did Will. Paul took a pull from an imported beer while Faye and Audra sipped on Caesars. Audra ordered snacks and before long, the gang was digging into a huge plate of spicy chicken wings. As Julie snapped pictures, Will mugged for the camera with a wide-open goofy grin reminiscent of the Muppets. Later, a close friend of Audra and Paul's, Greg Scratchley, handed Paul a birthday card. His birthday is in August, so some people at the table were confused. Greg smiled. It's a RE-birthday card, he said. One year ago today, Paul was reborn.

>>>

THE FRANKLIN FAMILY MADE AN IMPORTANT journey as the anniversary of the suicide bombing approached. Shortly before Christmas 2006, Audra and Paul, together with Simon and Faye,

From the left, Will, Jeff, and Paul at Fisher House in Landstuhl, Germany, in December 2006.

Photo credit: Franklin family archive

travelled back to the military hospital in Landstuhl. Paul and Audra brought a gift to present to the people who ran Fisher House, the family hostel that had welcomed Audra, Faye, and Simon in January 2006. The hostel staff and volunteers provided comfort and support, not to mention clean sheets and home-cooked meals. The Franklins wanted to say thank you.

In an outpouring of sympathy, Canadians had offered money to the Franklins to help the family recover after Paul was injured. That's when Audra came up with the idea of giving the money to Fisher House. After receiving permission from the military, which closely monitored all offers of help from the public, Audra began to collect donations. She organized a fundraising dinner and silent auction in Edmonton to raise money for the hostel. In total, the Franklins collected eighty thousand dollars. The Franklins, together with Will and Jeff and members of their families who also stayed at Fisher House, travelled to Germany for the cheque presentation.

While in Landstuhl, Audra met a young woman who reminded her of herself a year earlier. The woman's husband, an American soldier, had lost his legs in Iraq after an improvised explosive device destroyed his Humvee. One of the soldier's legs had been amputated above the knee, the other below the knee.

"I could see exactly where we started and how scary it was. You didn't know whether they would be waking you in the middle of the night to say you have to come. It was just really scary and I could see that on her face," Audra said. "And then I thought about how it is for us now. I really saw that. I looked at Paul and thought: We've gone this far now."

By any outward measure, Paul and Audra have made a remarkable comeback. They have pulled themselves and their son through a family crisis. They have planted trees in the backyard of their new home and raised funds for other amputees in need. Paul has flown to Vancouver and Winnipeg to comfort other wounded soldiers and their families. Countless military spouses, those with injured partners and those who just need a few words of support, have contacted Audra. She tries to respond to all of the calls and e-mails.

"People are looking to us for a lot of guidance, for help. Being part of the healing of everybody else keeps us quite busy. But I think it's a help to us."

Some aspects of their lives feel better than they did before the suicide bomb attack. Audra enjoys having a new and bigger home. She and Paul have been travelling more, and meeting new people. Audra was thrilled with an invitation to sit at Michaelle Jean's table at the Governor General's gala ball in June 2006. Unfortunately, she suffered a migraine headache at the event and spent most of the evening in another room, drinking ginger ale and eating crackers. She made it back to the table in time for dessert.

"The Governor General patted my hand and said, 'You're here for the best part,'" she remembered.

Audra did not go back to work after finishing a contract in the summer of 2006. Working at home with Simon has enriched her relationship with her son, who is recovering well from the family trauma. His marks in school have bounced back to where they were before his father's injury. Simon is a straight-A student who receives positive comments from his teachers on his report card. Big crowds and lots of noise upset him. At school, he wears an MP3 player. He listens to music while he works at his desk to drown out the distractions of the world around him.

Instead of working full-time, Audra has launched a home-based event-planning company with a girlfriend. Organizing the Landstuhl fundraiser, as well as events for Red Friday—a national movement to encourage wearing red to show support for Canadian troops overseas—proved to her that she has a talent for pulling it all together. She hopes she can turn the skill into a profitable

Simon is excited to sit in the cockpit of the plane on the way to Germany during a family trip to Landstuhl in December 2006.

Photo credit: Franklin family archive

business. Her friend Barb says Audra has "taken a lump of coal and turned it into a diamond with everything she and Paul have done. Other people would say, 'Where is my help?' But she are Paul are just doing it."

Audra and Paul are closer as a couple in some ways than they were before the explosion. Audra knows her husband better. In the last year, Paul has allowed her to see his vulnerable side, at least at home, something he never would have done before.

One day Paul was in his wheelchair at the kitchen table. Audra was bustling around the house, on her way out the door. She had her purse over her shoulder and car keys in hand. Paul stopped her.

"Don't go," he said. He looked at her, his eyes steady.

"Oh. Well. Okay." She put down her purse and pulled up a chair. It was just a moment, but it was a different moment than they had known before.

This is not a time of tidy conclusions and happy endings. Audra has fears for the future that cannot be soothed.

"I'm scared Paul will be released from the military. He's supposed to be released. And what if he doesn't get a job afterwards, what if there's no market for his speaking, something that he really wants to do? What if he can't get a job as a (tactical medicine) teacher, something else that he really wants to do? I worry about him having a fulfilling life after the military is done and after the hullabaloo goes away."

Audra is still so very tired. Paul takes care of himself and is in many ways independent, but his wife has a lot to do alone. Heaving the wheelchair into the trunk. Hauling the bottles and cans out to the back alley for recycling. Sometimes Audra gets mad at Paul for not trying hard enough to do those guy things that have felt awkward to him since he lost his legs. Barbecuing reminds him of the man he was and he does not want that reminder. Audra tells him she does not want to barbecue either, but somebody has to do it.

"Paul was always the guy who'd get up in the middle of the night and investigate the noise. I always felt safe with him. And now I don't. Now I think I'm the one who provides the safety. Roles have definitely switched. He used to shut the house up at night. He was always in bed after me. Now I have to shut the house up before I go to bed because he can't reach certain things in the house. Or if Simon's asleep downstairs, I have to carry him up. Normally Paul would have done that."

Audra says her husband has become a different person. He is not as patient and has no time for people who complain, even Simon.

"Simon will say, 'Oh, my legs hurt because I'm growing,' and Paul will say, 'Well, at least you have legs.' He is a very different man. Not only physically, obviously, but emotionally, he's very different."

"It's hard. It's hard. It's hard."

Paul acknowledges he has changed; that was unavoidable.

"Every tour is the same. The wives talk about how their husbands have changed. Well, you bet they change, and with wounded soldiers, it's the same thing. I've seen and done things that were amazing, horrible, all of that. And you change through that."

Like Audra, Paul worries about his ability to support his family over time. He recently signed another contract with the military for service until 2009, so he doesn't need to think about a new career for now. At the end of this contract, Paul will be eligible for a pension of 20 per cent of his annual salary of fifty thousand dollars as a master corporal. That's on top of his veteran's disability pension. Paul thinks about teaching other medics, or starting a consulting business to advise companies with employees working overseas in dangerous locales. He has accepted numerous speaking engagements across Canada and he hopes a career as a motivational speaker will emerge.

"I do have a new fear of me failing for the future, failing for my son and my wife. I worry that I'll be that person who just tells old stories and doesn't do anything with his life. That's my biggest fear now. My biggest fear is that I won't be able to provide properly as a good husband and father."

Daily practical issues remain. Aside from learning to walk, Paul has other physical challenges. Pain is always with him. He may spend his life on some amount of morphine. He is not yet used to his new body and talks to his psychologist and to his wife about this difficulty. He and Audra are struggling to re-establish sexual intimacy. Paul says the reluctance comes more from him than from Audra. Though Paul is proud of his body in some ways—his abs are better than ever—he is shocked when he sees himself in a full-length mirror. "That's a killer. I break down then." Paul wants to take the full-length mirror down from behind the bedroom door. Audra thinks it should stay because Paul needs to accept his body.

The future of a marriage is often a question mark for couples, and it's no different for Paul and Audra. Sometimes Audra worries they won't make it, but she doesn't talk to Paul about that. He doesn't mention his secret fears to her either. They have enough to worry about right now and it is risky to raise this visceral issue.

"I'm scared it isn't going well and that there will be problems that will keep surfacing to the point where they can't be corrected," Paul says. "And I'm afraid she doesn't love the person I am now. But I don't know what to do about that. I can't worry about that right now. My focus is recovery."

Paul's goal is to return to being the man he was on January 12, 2006, the day he hiked up the mountain in Afghanistan.

"Everything I did on that day is what I want to be able to do someday. It will take a long time to get there and a lot of effort. But I'm way past where I should have been. At this point, normal people would maybe have been using a walker, but not crutches, not canes. If I can scramble up the side of a mountain, I can do anything. That's when I'll stop striving."

The Franklin family in their living room in May 2007.

Photo credit: Ian Scott

Sometimes Audra forgets what has happened to her and to her family. It usually happens during the night. A soothing wave of dreams dissolves her fear and anxiety. In the morning, lying in her warm bed, her body soft and heavy against the mattress, Audra's mind floats nowhere in particular as she wakens. Then slowly, truth lands. Without opening her eyes, Audra becomes aware that beside the bed is a wheelchair, and her husband has to use it. She rises and walks barefoot to the bathroom and notices the holders in the bathtub, where Paul puts his gel liners after he has washed them. Audra finds all of these reminders of her new life, every morning, before she has even brushed her teeth.

Paul thinks about the words of the journalist and amputee Michael Weisskopf, who says that American veterans who have had limbs amputated share a common trait. They struggle for identity. "The psychological scars of amputation ran deeper than those from conventional wounds of war. The blasts took away something deeply personal," Weisskopf writes in *Blood Brothers*. "None of us felt like the men who had gone to Iraq. We possessed the same minds; they just resided in different bodies."

Paul, too, feels a loss that goes beyond his limbs. He wishes he could find a way to fill an aching gap.

"I've left something in Afghanistan and I don't know what it is, besides my legs. Something inside me is missing. And a lot of people say that they have to go back. I'd love to go back. And I don't know why."

ACKNOWLEDGEMENTS

MANY PEOPLE HELPED WITH THIS CHALLENGING PROJECT. Most of all, I want to thank Paul, Audra, and Simon Franklin for their time and patience and for making me so welcome in their home. Faye Marshall, Audra's mother, and Ron and Barb Franklin, Paul's parents, were also liberal with their time and memories. Many of Paul and Audra's friends and military colleagues generously agreed to interviews, and Amy Pennington in particular spent hours talking with me.

Numerous members of Paul's health care team also spoke to me about their experiences with his recovery. I would like to thank Sandra Huculak of the Capital Health Authority in Edmonton for introducing me to the doctors, nurses, and other health professionals at the University of Alberta Hospital and the Glenrose Rehabilitation Hospital. I respect and admire all of Paul's dedicated caregivers, who worked hard to help him to walk again.

The first spark for this book emerged in a feature story about Paul and his family that I wrote for *The Edmonton Journal* in May 2006. *Journal* photographer Bruce Edwards worked with me on that project. His sensitive and powerful portraits are a huge contribution to this longer account of Paul's story, and I appreciate them. I am also grateful to *The Edmonton Journal* for giving me permission to publish the photographs again.

I want to thank my editors at *The Edmonton Journal* for their support on this project, and I am grateful to my deskmates for listening to me as I worked through the process of writing the book proposal and finding a publisher. A number of people were extra helpful, including English professor Ted Bishop of the University of Alberta; journalists Graham Andrews, Richard Helm, Terry McConnell, Maureen Palmer, Graham Thomson, and Sheila Pratt; and lawyer and author Karl Wilberg. My colleagues at CBC television also contributed to the project. I want to thank producer Jim MacQuarrie, as well as reporter Andreé Lau and producer Corinne Seminoff, for passing along interview transcripts from Andreé and Corinne's excellent documentary about Paul, which appeared on CBC's *The National*.

My husband, Ian Scott, spent many hours unravelling the mysteries of my computer, and I deeply appreciate his help. I would also like to thank my sons, Dylan and Daniel Zimmerman, for making me laugh, as always, and my parents, Betty and Bill Faulder, just because.

Finally, I am grateful to the Canadian Forces for allowing Paul to take part in this project when it would have been easier to say no. Katie McLaughlin in public affairs at Edmonton Garrison was patient and helpful, as were many public affairs officers in Ottawa.

I cannot begin to thank Ruth Linka of Brindle & Glass for giving a journalist a chance to explore an important story in more depth. Editor Linda Goyette was beside me all the way, and her thoughtful comments made this a better book.

LIANE FAULDER is an award-winning feature
writer with the *Edmonton Journal*. Liane's work
has taken her to Romania, where she reported on
the plight of orphans after the fall of Ceausescu,
and to Bosnia, where she wrote about Canadian
peacekeepers. Liane has been a regular contributor
to CBC radio, and has written for *Chatelaine*, *Today's
Parent*, and *Alberta Venture Magazine*. In 2006, her
personal essay, "About the Boys," was published
in the best-selling anthology of women's writing,
Dropped Threads 3. In 2007, Liane was awarded the
prestigious Canadian Journalism Fellowship at the
University of Toronto's Massey College.